BLEED THROUGH

BLEED THROUGH

NEW AND SELECTED POEMS

Michael Davidson

COFFEE HOUSE PRESS
MINNEAPOLIS 2013

COPYRIGHT © 2013 by Michael Davidson
COVER AND BOOK DESIGN by Linda Koutsky
AUTHOR PHOTOGRAPH © Sophia Davidson

COFFEE HOUSE PRESS books are available to the trade through our primary distributor, Consortium Book Sales & Distribution, cbsd.com or (800) 283-3572. For personal orders, catalogs, or other information, write to: info@coffeehousepress.org.

Coffee House Press is a nonprofit literary publishing house. Support from private foundations, corporate giving programs, government programs, and generous individuals helps make the publication of our books possible. We gratefully acknowledge their support in detail in the back of this book. To you and our many readers around the world, we send our thanks for your continuing support.

Visit us at coffeehousepress.org.

LIBRARY OF CONGRESS CIP INFORMATION
Davidson, Michael, 1944–
[Poems. Selections]
Bleed through : new and selected poems / by Michael Davidson.
pages ; cm.
ISBN 978-1-56689-339-8 (PBK.)
I. Title.
PS3554.A9257B57 2013
811'.54—DC23
2013003666
PRINTED IN THE U.S.A.
FIRST EDITION | FIRST PRINTING

ACKNOWLEDGMENTS
I would like to thank Marjorie Welish for her generous support and encouragement of this publication. I would also like to thank the editors of books from which these poems have been selected: Jack Shoemaker, Geoff Young, Rosemarie and Keith Waldrop, Stephen Ratcliffe, and Leslie Scalapino. Thanks are extended as well to the publishers of magazines in which many of the new poems in this volume first appeared.

FOR MARJORIE WELISH

New Poems

FROM "Chronic"

And every time I say, I said this, or, I said that, or speak of a voice saying, far away inside me, Molloy, and then a fine phrase more or less clear and simple, or find myself compelled to attribute to others intelligible words, or hear my own voice uttering to others more or less articulate sounds, I am merely complying with the convention that demands you either lie or hold your peace.

—SAMUEL BECKETT

New Poems

1998–2012

ANNIVERSARY

Are we crossing over
on this ship of Allegri
into the visible, hands
bearing the *Miserere*

across what decibels
waving from shore,
this populous air
of mouths open, intention

to speak
a kind of sky,
knitting the social
as a prow

made with hands
could cleave
clear water, when
did the Annunciation

of silence
first sound
by
what sign?

VACANT WEATHER

for Tom Raworth

I'm left holding the door,
the epitome walks through
an invisible version who salutes
this vestige or prosthesis

but generally materializes
in vacant air,
rising levels of abstraction
leave the head

empty, eyes gritty with amnesia
once defended against
by memorization, Polonius's
speech to his son

in the old folks' home,
or those lines in which mercy
becomes redundant,
"you see," he pauses in the slow lane

and addresses rapt thousands
in the rearview,
and we do; the king is in his counting
house doling out desire,

I'm still holding the door, still
born in the grid, it's getting expensive
to live in a world of light,
dark lines form at the margins

and students wrap themselves
around an eraser,
be true to your school,
phantom limb of yourself

I feel pain from a distance,
these thoughts occur in stress,
one for the street
and one the street displaces

count your blessings
as the rain comes on
patient measure
of vacant weather.

THE FRIEND

Last night was in waves and veils
that rounded waking into walking
through these corridors
without edges or counters,
I was somewhere there was something,
you were there in several sizes,

you could put your finger on a map
and the blank house, dead room
would return to a landscape,
and the incident with streetcars
or piers would connect
with a vacation in Spain, dancers
at the Avalon,

yet walking through streets
in the broad syntax of daylight
these mesa dwellings, wedges
of darkness, refuse to give in,
recalcitrant Freud, friend, friable
youth we hold these things to be pointed;

the friend has turned away
the wife has joined the army

the child looks to neighbors
for music, I must be a piano
of doubt, so many play

these gavottes on my back,
even the pronoun is laced with lime
as you pack it, ball and powder,
into a long gun, fire
and the report knocks you dead.

BAD MODERNISM

Suddenly all is / loathing.
—JOHN ASHBERY

and there's plenty to be unhappy about
if I can just get the reception area festooned
in time for their arrival, paper cups
and those little plastic whatsits so that,
gorged on meaning,
they troop through the glass doors
seeking interpretation, first floor
mildly historical, second floor
desire matrix, parents accompany
their indiscretions straight
to the penthouse, and someone
hands them a phone, "turtles"
they're called, heads bobbing
as though they had a choice
to be party favors, deep structure
on your left, follow the clicking
to a white cube, we only work
part-time, the other part
we illustrate profound malaise,
I like these cream-filled versions
so unlike what we get at home,
having said which

we rewind the tape,
slip it through a slot marked "aha"
and take the El home,
the smell you smell afar
is something boiling over.

BAD MODERNISM: THE WHITE CITY

When the rotor hums for a long time
among the gawkers
I fall into a ghost trance
and become a white man again;
nothing must penetrate this history
because nothing can be distinguished
from itself, down
on Midway Plaisance, amid the lights,
the dark beauties offer darkness, the eyes
go there while the will stands still,
in the Hall of Dynamos
the dead warriors will return
in a language no one remembers,
they have a stall in the Pavilion of Silence,
the ears go there
searching for treaties, tales of the elders,
from up here
the land is all parcels
like one of the new paintings,
nothing penetrates this illusion, prose
covers the brown earth
and in the hum of its scroll
can be heard a crowd of the visitors
clamoring at the entrance
with their tickets
to the white city.

BAD MODERNISM: SOUVENIR

the Garden of Allah is unknown to the senses

Douglas Fairbanks Sr.
flies over minarets,
you can almost see the wire,

he smiles while looking down,
she's having the ride of her life,
later, as Susannah

at the well
her alabaster will startle
cigar smoke in Secaucus

produce a sense of height
the sense of money and the other
brocades that assist intimacy,

an artist on Hudson
paints the Holy Land
as it stretches to Poughkeepsie

sun gilding the Berkshires
like light on an odalisque,
these arabesques make one almost

9

intimate, as the night comes down
drawn by camels,
the explosion could be heard

as the absent one
raised his glass
and the building fell on children

and the dust blew across the street,
by these slaves naked in the bazaar
we have entered the modern

the capitol dome
sports a fez
the Shriners wave from a float.

BAD MODERNISM: INTERSTICES

We're between rationalism and whatever is left out,
stuff caught in the drain, sex in the park
where it threatens to rain, the war
drains the state of excess
and leaves a hard residue of cash on the sill,
we spend it in spectacular restaurants
with nothing not green, nothing but grass,
the new owner greets us with something amber
and amuse-bouches on a plate, there's Kant
in the corner, wave to him honey,
it makes the trip from the Valley
seem a minute in a mall;

there was the Dual Monarchy
but that didn't last, then came the partition
and the annexations, new colonies
that became the old estates
and they brought out new epaulettes
and paraded them in the renamed square,
it's hard to catch up once you've begun
the long division, I remember now
we're between civilization and discontent
there's one of them now, turning his fork
through a reasonable salad;

if it weren't for the password
no one would enter paradise, there are so many
passwords I forget how to bludgeon myself
into a primitive hut in the name of something
once flame-like, insistent, piercing
the heart, passing a window in a moving train
we see ourselves as our fathers
no wonder we reach for the red handle
and send cars screeching into the ravine,
anything to avoid this inexorable motion
and the docent who appears
to explain it.

THINKING MANAGEMENT

I'm on a short line
but go ahead with your figures
and I'll double check
the delay quota

to see if something cruel
comes out the other end,
I was thinking Pyrrhus
or maybe the Falklands, something

small that has consequence,
acetylene spilled in a corn
field might get their
attention, black grass

and then this marina project
comes through
and we've got agents
walking the halls,

I tell you, if it weren't
for distance I'd be real;
my advice: don't say anything
you wouldn't want upstairs

to know, the lines
are full of eyes, money
goes one way but
we won't say it as such.

SUN

We are blinking in sunlight
our neighbors smoke next to the dish
they have converted into a birdbath,
buttermilk sky named after a song

as far away
as Ho Chi Minh, uncle
almost ephemeral like adolescence
(cancel reservation) plums

could be eaten in the tree
where sky dipped down
the higher you climbed,
youth had not been invented

along with television and Zimbabwe,
we were closer to the sun
and therefore immortal,
smoke drifts

across the contested fence
like these tufts of rhetoric
by which I arrange the desk
in preparation for eternal life,

to swim at dawn to the far buoy
and then look back at the life
guard tower is to see General MacArthur
returning again and again

to the beach, it is good to return
to these flecked surfaces
through which the sun
writes a letter, summer has come

and gone back into the closet
as the wind rises, I see
three dolphins
breaking the water.

POOR YORICK

I'm in receipt of these formula missives
that washed in with the tide
and littered the littoral, provoking
troop leader to jeremiad:

ballast of comfort, bloated Mc
national simulcast soundbyte
and deregulated spam filter public option
for public shared with . . .

the histories they recount have left their listeners
blanched, but the damage they inflict
on this card house of rectitude
endures in the late-night sweats

when they play the uncut version,
I was once you, but you have detached
yourself from my invention
to take up the pen

and write back
in a sputtering apostrophe,
a voluntary of indignation that casts its shade
on my adamantine torso,

Dead Head of the Pope, Eye of Cyclops
then came the "deaf" period
followed by Gainsborough
Shepherd Boys with Dogs Fighting,

from a distance we thought they were mangos
or shipwrecked papaya, how disappointing
to find the Duomo under scaffold
(open file, select "dust")

their subject is Rome, imperium
among vassals and migrants
still crossing the Alps in search
of technology and healthcare,

nothing changes but the quality of rage
you anticipate in the smile
once seen among the middling sorts
where everyone has lost her accent,

first light, lost friend,
send key, find map,
the person I was born with
is walking the ramparts

with the person he was dying to become
please stay on the line
and the next representative
will represent you.

THE PUBLIC SPHERE

There's a lot to be said for celibacy
no sudden actions or alarms,
a crowd is attached to the spleen
the liver waves from the beach,

first the blue horizon was visible through pines
then it was obliterated by the modified plan
although palms mitigated the view corridor
until they drilled a hole in a hall,

we held yellow triangles to our chests
to offset the strawberries on theirs, parking
was at a premium, mud flaps
at half-mast,

when the marshal divided the room
with yellow tape there were low growls
coming from the augurs, let's throw
a chicken to the sea, what do the entrails say,

I can see it from their perspective:
young couples in coupes arrive from Tucson
to witness excess in erect bodies,
it brings in revenue and they become not us,

bodies, broken,
bruised, bent out of
and into shape the
slope of a spine, the
curve of a wrist, the
bleeding edge of all
these bodies, obsessed with physical
forms, the only thing)
we truly feel

19

I see two of them now by the window
consuming colored waters in goblets
until the sun amazes an anesthesiologist
by dissolving into pain,

you don't get wet
and pay on your way out.

THE ASSUMPTION

Although I populate and attend conferences
I am not without significant borders; although I require medication
and sleeping attire I am prepared to travel long distances
and engage uncomfortable portage; last year
I was embarrassed to find myself the afflatus
among wilted cauliflower and dour turkey roulades,
this year I can no longer observe my knees
retreating from their customary indecision
whether to stand or kneel as befits a senator
before an oil rig; last night
there were luminaries at the table, I was handed
the list and made subtle movements
known only to the waiter, music
disturbs my sleep, and I spend much of the night
banging on the wall for assurance
that these squeaks of ardor are not sighs
of the assassin spreading his mulch of anxiety
in a field of pumpkins; swelling violins,
I think I can speak for all of us, intimate
those lost bedsits and furtive afghans
in attached garages as we expand
before the font, the misery of grout
in a tile countertop brings us back
to these shattered alveoli, Golgi bodies

that we share with newts, my project this year

is to make of this hollowed crèche

a more perfect assumption

that you could take with you

in a canoe, the viola signals that it's time

for them to close the casement

in a room used only on formal occasions

of which this

has been merely a prospectus.

THE RAPTURE

"He's back! He's back!" her husband Everett said
she said just before she climbed through the sunroof
and jumped off the moving car, causing a twenty-car pileup
outside Little Rock; Everett said she saw Jesus
standing by the side of the road
and twelve disciples floating in the air;
as it turns out, wind
blew the tarp off a truck, and twelve blow-up sex dolls
filled with helium lifted into the sky,
the long-haired driver, on his way to a toga party,
pulled over, got out, looked up,
lifted his arms into heaven; she was dead.
When asked why his wife would do such a thing, Everett
replied, "I think my wife loved Jesus more than she loved me."

ARCADIA

Now that the outline is complete
I need to omit everything,
the fence and the prepositions
that bring me to the fence

reserving one page for the whiteness
beyond resolve
that appears in the late sonatas
as an extended aria

almost vanishing
yet returning by packet
to turn yourself in
for crimes pursued in insomnia,

they construct Arcadia just in time
for the fall sales
and you have a small stall
next to the enthymemes

by which the will to contain everything
will succeed
and the money left over
can be given to charity,

when they turned off the loudspeakers
God was still speaking
of his accomplishments
and the crowd wouldn't leave,

I have a record of it here
somewhere, the papers
resemble leaves and the leaves
are becoming fire.

THE TROUT

The act of waiting
or the art of watching
were the pediments
of this parenthesis

having lost his notes, the transfer
or the phone number, glasses
so weak
that he sought a passerby

to read the fine print
of a schedule the terminus of which
remained obscure and the vehicle
in which he was to ride

through mountains, a high
fjell only to descend
into a purple city made
out of rain

in the mist
and the beloved who now
it appears
would turn away from the station

and return to the apartment alone,
their meaning dissolved into sequence
to be effaced entirely
and so erase the illusion

of itself as the end
of waiting or watching
and the sullen river roiling
under the bridge

on which tourists gather
in the afternoon
to watch silver trout
feeding on bread, they

must be necessary
to the mountains as
the system and the boy
in a red hat

support this caesura nothing
can fill, perpetually vanishes
bearing its witness.

THE BODY AND THE PICTURE OF THE BODY

In the middle of summer
maybe in the middle of middle
everything silences,
even the freeway has rolled back
into its sibilance
and dogs inhabit the sofa
looking interested
without doing much about it,
we miss you in Boston, in Maui,
in far-off Sandpoint, the waves
shimmer, what else do they have
to do when merged with wind,
I imagine you down at the dock
staring into water, small explosions
in the distance
remind us how perfect memory
used to be, a rock
becomes a trout, skitters away
because war is as timeless
as doubt is close to the sun,
you unwrap the heavens
and place them next to each other,
and they invent Hell
to be under everything,

our leaders say don't go out,

extremity waits under the larches

for innocence not

to discover itself,

words are perfect,

we can put perfection into a report

and say fire is a hot liquid,

names a conspiracy of clerks,

I used to remember the names of

those things next to the rock,

flowers I think, grasses and inner tubes

chairs and flashlights, miracle

of the truly contingent

through which you dive

in the utterly useless and necessary heat.

irrelevant at times irrelevant,
the world exploding into pieces at the seams
adolescence surprising us still
we forget to breathe, dive
into this excess of wanting
leading scientists blame absintee parents
smoking among youths goes up
constantly searching for the next person
to drink with
drink up
trail off in the middle of sentences
god sometimes
when im on my knees i feel like i'm
burning up

29

THE CANADIANS

I'm going out on a limb here
words never fit the slots we paid for
in advance
so you stuff them with your thumb
until a semblance of space and time
permits you to use the phone,
you dial up a rep
and listen to an ad for a new kind of card,
the snow rises above the fenders,
but you have time to substitute thyme
for rosemary, stuff the breast
and roast at 400,
loon north soft blue rain
pills, tractors, combines, apples
flowing south, wolves
circle the Armada
where we are embalmed in cold
hoping for access,
one of them signifies here and another
the place here vacates
like a retired couple
at the first frost, first
they pull back the lake
and expose the dock, purple

i read your words and
for a minute my blood
sings, hot, blue
and i have lived

sky, beached kayak, I want
to occupy what
has not been bought, the space
where the earth meets the earth.

practice denying ourselves
questions within our faith
always speaking in the plural
accidental assignment of meaning to simple
syntax
subtext, sensual touche escalates we feel
magnitude
take my coffee black
i don't deserve
my false martyrdom

aren't you now tired? or go
drop the pretense/
of the illusion
that your body wants anything
but comfort that
being touched doesn't
feel good that
his hands finally the line
of your leg lip?
doesn't keep you alive

CANON

There we were
dunning the manuscript
for all it was worth
wearing our white gloves
and parsing the stains
for signs of stress
following the divorce, an asterisk
where an obscure accident
prevented reveille being played
over your bier, the quays
where you found the key
to an inexplicable quatrain
simply hold back the river
whose bridges etched against blue
resemble almost anything
on page sixty-four, for example,
the large woman lifting her skirts
at Ocean Beach, the smell of lingerie
at Saks, everything you re-create at night
when they turn off
the amygdala remains preserved
in amber if you can remember
the first phoneme, catacombs
of crimes and misdemeanors
the canon upon which this scrawl
veers toward paradise.

WHITMAN

I think forth of the punctilious
and limitless mountains
that squeamish many another might
in nightshirts or gingham under the sway
and ballast of these portents infect
while gathering forward emulate
that states made of such half-timbered
and viperous rattle
that the constitution shivers withal
among stuff I proffer, unheeded
and gaunt or stifling in your
hot rooms or besmirched in britches
who read these leaded and cast lines
that we become fundament and igneous
in one Allegheny
at present we are environed with nonsense
and squeaks stifled neath bedcovers.

SUBURBS IN NOVEMBER

These leaves leave us as we are
in air, one day
the shed behind revealed,
one day difference moves from green
to red, the birds have given up
as the figs sag into scrotums
and Norma's smoke no longer wafts
across the feeder dish.

It was a momentary attempt
at writing something successful,
bad idea, winter surprised us
bare ruined choirs
that sort of farmer's market version
of health, utterly
efficient, no waste, the endorphins
pop with smug assurance,
the birds confirm an adage.

We can all go inside now,
back to the indispensible door
from which daily we reinvent
"we" as a familiar event
such as eating or swimming,

34

it's easier in a group to assign
colors to titles and titles
to someplace we keep forgetting,
passed along the highway in
Nevada or Oklahoma,
I remember Winnemucca
for the cat that escaped
but little else.

FOR RYDER

It's almost true
I'm in this mirrored room
sorting out the infinite excess of me
down that series of overtones, each
expanding the terms of this aperture
that is both blind and overcome with vision,
cancel my order,
you are there in a way
watching me attempt to climb around my image
so that I can see backstage, the ungainly props
and even the logo on the back
of your teeshirt, VRBO,
the unpronounceable action of capital in the infinitive
form that allows so many actors, and in two rooms
we sort out our dreaded parting
like a couple of molecules
that have decided to live in opposite bodies,
you take the subway home,
and I'll fly back to Normal Heights, the mirror
of solitude becomes the window of care
through which the tonic proffers endlessly
its hand, you can always return.

CREATIONISM

I'm slouching past the point of no
interruptions the planet dissolving
from its patented heat death; I, too,
watch this cryogenic state thaw
under the stare of the hedge fund,
black car shows up
and gives them a check, I scream
and the sprinklers pulsate
in a thousand yards
because grass is not inevitable
but symptomatic, take my gene pool
all is smooth, no regrets,
and once this gazebo is swept
another will take its place or
no one will notice, a frog
appears on the fountain's ledge
singing its two-beat refrain
it says I'm going in that direction
and I adapt.

sixteen and obsessed with sex
shame too
biting my lip, in a modest shirt
i am thinking of something
obscene
love making is a weak word for someone
pretending to be hard edges
my mouth doesn't trip up 37 on the word fucking
i do not believe in a higher power

DON'T SAVE

I'm not angry, just curious,
a key lost in an argument
remains a cloud in the shape of a
question, what follows
erases the cause and substitutes
a car, a bunch of chard, charity
joins these proteins glowering
at each other in the doorway,
they resonate like family
or famine, a blank interval
in which investments achieve body
and accrue interest, I'm guiltless
because I invent the bank
and the ones who wish you a nice day,
it's a small price
for the explosion that follows.

CEREAL

I'd rather bleed
than pay taxes,
sitting in the dark
with my gun against
the gathering dawn
I speak English
in my dreams,
dawn reveals a field
of agents measuring
the story poles, my camera
captures them
with my cereal,
we're eating our way
through subsidies,
corn is oil is cow,
I remain stubbornly
open and invested
in tracts that promise
golf, but people who walk
in parks must be hunted,
asked politely to leave
as a sycamore
bears a white slash
as its visa
these big words
trouble my sleep,

my suit is pressed
into public service
as my wife
removes her body
before waking,
I have eaten my cereal
without sweetener
and with advancing light
raise my sights
to those hordes
and indigestible foods
that occupy my eye
I trust no one
to remove these dishes
no one to speak
for me, what I keep
to myself is to myself
the sound of mice
in the rafters
is mine, solitude
has been described
in a book
it says do not become
excessive, digressive
be thou me in short
and let neighbors
bury their cats.

THE UNCANNY

Seeks advice on how to get home
(sacrifice, ritual toast, drink blood) where home
(we want to get some of that love) is big business,
I feel ephemeral in the shadow of logo,
it keeps drawing me into an agreement I authored,
they say: I feel anxious about my body, I worry
about my general health, work
sets you free, and when money
replaces a doorstop, potatoes, dog food
then we improve (it says here),
achieving a plural of such substance
as to wake the sleeper
who lives in broadband limbo, connected
yet unsure who is at the door, rituals inoculate
the viewer from choice, knock
on wood.

little boy all the girls
you date
look like your mother
and the princesses you
saw on tv
i am so much
grown up the first time
someone called me
a bitch and i
realized i did not
have to listen

the first time, this one is mine

41

GRACE

While billeted among participial
and other progressive forms
frames of indiscretion recombine
into plausible stories of origin
so that upon becoming grammar
one hypothetically strikes one's forehead
on a sentence striving to form itself
into the subject, capital *S*,
the residue of tower, codex, and ceremonial
song to explain these barriers to terminus
recur intermittently during the day
so that upon meeting him halfway home
one would never know what bullets
penetrate the memory theater, striking
a patron as inconceivable to the plot
and necessary to language, whereupon
he concludes this little tale
of our first parents, burnished in grace.

REBARBATIVE

I repudiate *rebarbative*,
a word surrounded by microbes
wanting to enter the enigma like an asteroid
and causing panic among the follicles
followed by a fluid emitted
at the first sign of coagulation,
naming is a queer connection
between a missing arm and its ghostly pain
that the word excites when encountered
in a trench or under a bridge,
I was once a whole name
in a neighborhood of partials,
I remembered their faces
from the photos attached to their chests:
you were the one "with hair,"
you were known as "the diver,"
many meanings have traveled to Asia
where, refreshed, they reemerge in Kensington,
their lanterns
a panopticon of nostalgia, Penny Lane
a clean machine, even when the lyrics fade
the space they occupied returns in a float,
over there
we had an Asia you could pay people to sweep,

the first you ever breathed
was a word
embers, ash
not the fire you brought
but what came after
the torn edges of lettuce
paper, made to a perfect
square
they always said you
had forethought
did you know how
the iron would feel
when it pinned you
how sharp those
claws would be
the visceral red
purple of your liver
did you know it
would be worth it?

43

no-can-do anymore, the digital link
rejects the teahouse, Pinkerton
is applauded in Houston
while Bechtel rebuilds a bank,
we have been in this place for going on
nine hundred years and still
I get a kick out of language,
it's so like

FROM

The
Mutabilities

1976

I am watching the vanguard move in,
it speaks from the everywhere it has left
and takes everyone by surprise
even though they have waited for spring
for a thousand years; we need it
and its winds will raise the hair on our necks
before any leaf has begun to quiver;
already we hear the melody in the violins
and observe the swimming that precedes drowning,
"More room!" he cries to the empty covenants
where the lightning flashes over the plain,
a great gray front with hunched shoulders
sends all of the fathers scurrying like ants
from a flooded ant hole; the grammar
displaces families instantly upon contact; I am
not afraid of its words or the power of connections
by which the sky is mottled and the sea is gray;
I am waiting while the last red carnations
drag their heads, forgetting all they call
to mind in my grandmother's memory,
they are the last
and the fiction of their scent
has made her faint with joy
for the first and last time,
now she is speaking from Nova Scotia, from England,
from Ireland and where will she go next?

Never to return to it, just as well,
a gate in the garden opens a casket in hell,
she looks down, the child she beholds
she becomes, there are shelves
in the garden that want fixing,
they have been there since the beginning
and the long grass weaves in and out,
the shelves are not wanting, a conscience
wants to fill them
with objects likely to be broken,
yellow and blue, to rename
the garden and the door
to the child that lies peaceful and alone,
just as deep as the face found lovely
goes desire who waits for no man
who has no home.

LES VACANCES

This is clear. Letters omitted in playing music. They are all gone up into the realms of light: clear air, harpsichord, lack of dynamics, determined space, half geography (interference), half mind (as they say, "half-witted," which has always suggested one poor at jokes; I myself have felt lost in space at the urging of a punch line and from now on will appear only in parenthesis) bracketing densities like an outfielder, arranging accidents on the backs of cigarette cards:

> e.g., leg peppered with shot
> foreign body trapped in ear
> burning woman

He sits there all day buttressed around by cats and gifts and music. On the outside all appears complex, but on the inside the air is condensed like a single tone that extends for the duration of a normal human scream.

Last night they saw *Mildred Pierce* with Joan Crawford and observed the beauty of balustrade, doorknob, and rounded fender. "Where do you live?" she asks. "By my ocean," he replies.

"I was hiding behind screens since before you were born!" says Bette Davis. The grillwork is dense. Each phrase is heard from the war as well as from the vantage of the present. The theme of the movie (and of his visit) is the recurrence of the present in the life of one living for the future. The lack of vowels blocks credences, gardens glutted by rain, dogs, puddles standing for weeks. How old could she be to be her daughter? The faith in blond curls.

EIGHT STATEMENTS FOR JOAN FROM JOHN

Better watch out! There is nothing we like so much to communicate to others as the seal of secrecy—along with what lies under it.
—NIETZSCHE

1. There is an unalterable purpose to evasion not unlike the fortuitous discoveries made along the way to curing a disease. What they tell you about one's present health is never so valid as what they tell you about the health one has had. In this sense, like Zeno's Achilles, we never arrive at the destination our discoveries limit.

2. The assignment was to write "about" the act of thinking and without reference to the "object" of one's thought. The result was a series of confrontations with metaphor.

3. She had heard through a friend that he had spoken of her lack of seriousness in conversation. He remembered having spoken of the formal interview in which seriousness is a requisite fact, one of its unasked questions. In reality what the friend had misinterpreted was the case, brought suddenly into relief by her righteous anger.

4. How to achieve the effect of wholly unmediated speech without speaking. What the oracle expelled was a fine blue vapor known for its narcotic properties. Hence what the seeker sought was not the truth but the ecstasy that the truth suggested.

5. In order to discover the city made out of old poems it was necessary to destroy the first seven walls surrounding it.

6. John and Ann stroke the cat between them. His indecision over the meaning of simple phrases prevents him from generating sentences.

7. The meaning of simple phrases lies in the validity as meaningful units within larger units called sentences. "(B)etween them" is as ambiguous as "John and Ann."

8. She was a fast reader. The text moved past her eyes like the train in the Michelson–Morley experiment. Actually, the train was used as a metaphor only when someone was walking within it. The text stands for something that moves at varying rates of speed depending upon who is reading it.

The voice would come intermittently into the Bartok so that it became part of the music. It was the voice of one who explains something of the weather to airplanes, something of the sea surface to ships, something of people in numbers to cruising police. It had a purpose like the music. But what he took from the combination was a third intent, a third theme that concerned what she had said earlier about how she was to meet this other friend the next night for a drink. This was part of their plan, the meeting of diverse persons with whom relationships were possible. Their relationship, while being of some duration and weight, seemed unassailable by this plan. But the messages go out into the night as warnings, often as interruptions of the music that plays slightly ahead of our ability to grasp it.

THE FEELING TYPE AND HIS FRIENDS

He cannot imagine a doorknob,
it comes off in his hands,
the golden doors designed to provoke
an end to writing
stand unopened, signs
rally behind the market,
all approaches are green and yellow
hitchhiking over the Sierras,
yet he has lost all feeling
and the beautiful cortege
will remember him in Reno,
flags bristling against the desert
while he reads the marks
in the pavement
and the sounds they make
are the voices of his friends
playing chess in the dark.

THE INTUITIVE TYPE AND HIS FRIENDS

Sad Young Man on a Train
grows no older than before
never wiser but something about her smile
wide as all Kansas

suggests the vase in five positions,

categories of doubt,

resonances of arch vaulting

and ubiquity of E-flat

in the sonata allegro form;

somewhere he hears a disparaging word

in a land with no language

but the deer and the antelope

know everything

and keep it to themselves.

THE SENSATION TYPE AND HIS FRIENDS

A button,

a basket of buttons, a cheese

a fat mama and bacon, a race

in the mountains, a glass

of young women;

he tries to forget everything,

along the way he picks up travelers

in specific directions,

they fill in the spaces

with what they've seen, a garden,

a stench of butter, a reeking

of stairways, old gaffers

hugging their treasures under the docks,

America bereft of depth
into you go I, He, We, It, She, and Them,
go touch what you asked us to give you,
a big bent fender,
a big rear ender.

THE THINKING TYPE AND HIS FRIENDS

Polish as in squash and gleam
depending on the irrepressible world
which opens its mouth like a grouper
or pin fish from which bubbles
are logical markers of depth
or "deaths" upon expiration
not accountable or likely
especially a small and compressed
dark-green grunt of the Atlantic coast
and everything is interesting
and we are all your friends.

He would like to avoid seeing himself
coming out of every door
but Jack was right,
he enjoyed suffering and knew
that they enjoyed it too.
The grammar here is confusing,
does he mean that they suffer
and derive pleasure
or is it his suffering that they enjoy?
It's a bland day
full of yellow rafts rocking
on an uncertain sea,
to do the wash without shame, to sink
a few baskets all in fun
and then go down to the beach
where they all have the semblance
of a good time,
who was Jack to tell him anything?
By golly,
he'd show him.

You didn't see how you got there
but once you were seated
they pulled the table away;

it's like this:
they wanted to see you as you are
and you wouldn't let them;

this is the story about everyone
wanting to be loved
and succeeding.

AFTER WHITEHEAD

The sequence is up in the air,
I'm outside or inside,
in each case
it's the truth
but who tells it
is up to the code
since it is green in two places
at once, air
is a solid wall
through which feathers float
like molten metal,
my father
is in all the dreams
I'm sure you've seen him,
now it is the second movement
and he's added a clarinet;
I lied,
it was a xylophone.

FROM

The Prose
of Fact

1981

TITLE

At the same time
next week
is a few degrees away,
but he thinks

it starts over,
the Bear slipping into place,
Orion lower
and to the right

and Sagittarius
whose month he is
has never seen
is to the south,

what connects us
is is
two forms
keeping their distance,

their conversations
with the Minotaur
have been recorded
have been recorded

PLATO'S CAVE

For this invention will produce forgetfulness in the minds of those who learn to use it because they will not practice their memory.

But how had he come to find it important enough if not because in trying to remember what one man had said of an earlier man on the subject of letters, which would have been lost to him had not this latter man invented the former for the purposes of remembering what he had said he had written it down? That takes care of that, he thought, adjusting his penwipe before proceeding. He had, after all, "thought," which to him meant filling the pen prior to writing and then "sowing" his seed with words that cannot defend themselves by argument and cannot teach the truth effectively. At least this is what he was told he was told he was told he was doing. Having accomplished thought, he could now begin to plant, as it were, the memory he would ultimately need in order to discover truth.

He thought of himself as the most abject and humble of men, walking about the agora in a musty robe, reeking of garlic, and yet here he was remembering the beginning of letters—his own, as it turned out—as he used them to accomplish fantastic and impossible things. For example, the example he had just used to forget what he'd been getting at. What *had* he been getting at? Some germ idea had been in his mind following dinner, and he had meant to interrogate it in the fashion of Lysias, but he had fallen prey to the mellifluous and honeyed quality of his own words and had lost the seed. But surely this was verification of what he had read of what another had said in his dialogue with a younger man who had just heard something and could only repeat it as he had remembered it. Ah, these orators know what they are remembering, he thought, and know what they know as well. Knowing this was better than writing it down, and it must have been in the satisfaction this recognition brought him that he fell asleep and dreamed of Thoth, Ibis imperious with a beak of ink, sower of dreams among dialecticians and rhetors alike.

AT LAST

The solution presented itself:
he'd simply stop talking,
she could invent anything she wanted
and he could confirm the nothing
upon which it was based
much as he had confirmed the everything
she expected through his words
by merely being in the room,
a kind of wind or small tremor
upon which the guests comment
"did you feel that?"
but silence is never silent,
the dog barks at insufficiency
which cries, siren-like,
and carries the burden of other voices,
lies, for example,
based on the truth they displace
are noisy in the middle of the night
before jactitation or orgasm or insomnia
like ghosts in a gothic novel,
but this silence would be perfect
like all perfections before the fact,
he'd be inscrutable, she'd be alarmed
but intrigued,

eventually the word "you"
would have to be erased,
the "I" that barricades himself
behind this strategy
has already started planning
by noticing the way she
avoids his eyes.

SUMMER LETTERS

The "i"s are skillful, distinguished and clever, have many pointed
weapons, and live in caves, between which, however, there are also moun
tains, gardens and harbors.
—MELANIE KLEIN

The *I*'s live in caves under the earth,
down here, it's summer
and hotter than anything else,

when it was winter
we did all the work,
and nobody disturbed us,

the letters were written
in the cool mornings
and by afternoon

they were received,
and nobody cared
how;

the *i*'s and *e*'s ride together
on a motor scooter;
they know where they are going

(into the wind probably),
they love one another
with a tenderness unknown

in the real world;
these are not my words
but those that summer gives me

in order to create love
as my cat creates another, larger cat
to hiss at,

"hiss" is made out of an agreement
between wind and tongue
not to recognize their limitations

the way memory and summer
reveal their terrible affinities
while speaking separate dialects,

I wish the poem of satisfaction
would write me a letter
as though I had written to E

in the full flush of their conjoining
as in neighbor and weigh
where friends share a sieve,

where there is little to remember
but stormy days
I would have a house of my own

words, and they would comfort
as you do
living between us,

for now, great uncertainty strides
across the film of sea
erasing all distinctions

I need
you fill
we move.

Tonight is closer than we thought (he meant to write "colder" but moved closer to the heater instead). The words on the way sounded like "bright star" and "hieroglyph" and "centaur" for the persistence of darkness surrounding brilliant outlines. Traversals of the room, of the lower heavens, of the traversals themselves in which wronged words fuse. He moved closer to the heater instead. It got hotter, and the words melted slightly into "heavens" and "aprons" and "arbors" for the continuity of darkness, spacing and pairing. The light so given to the room that the heavens are here, wearing their dark capes and bearing our outlines. We see through them as they shape and wrap these sensible things in aether and distance ("either endistanced," he heard) or a horse from a rider. I am the centaur at the edge of hemispheres. He wrote, simply, "spheres," and they melted.

BEFORE THE EVENT

In the sex light
he meant a street lamp
she glowed over roiling water
spread along a passage

from him to her
in the street the cars
rolled along the pavement,
he thought

to point her out
among the stars
her womb a cup
his cock the handle

simple blackness
with a plan
like a man about to
mean something.

DISCOVERING MOTION

Some things never get done
while others
just want you to be yourself,

there are so many numbers
affixed to the obligations they announce
that once you get on the bus

everyone will give you directions,
transfer at Barcelona
and head north into the Pyrenees,

because in order to complete the list
"home" is base
"money" the structure

and "mommy" is where the bus
can never take you,
some of the corners

come with signs and all the signs
say arrow,
where the houses run into the sea

you will discover motion.

VARIATIONS ON BENVENISTE
AND THE MASTER LIST

I am one who goes by the name of one,
        I speak the word ungarbled,
I am he whose name begins with *h*
        Mother of Voices, Black Swamp,
I announce myself as one who announces,
        Apple of Beauty and Discord,
I by being I remain eternally he,
        Thrilling Wonder Stories,
I am the speaker who is the speaker of I,
        Mysterious Barricades fall away,
Oh All, how I yearns to be you,
        to be taken up in your Society of Corresponding Fellows,
The pick, the arrow, and the wheel are not in nature
        but I am the one who wields them, you
        make me curiously strong, you
        indicate me,
And I am the echo of your you, the one
        who says you to me,
        Good Morning Teaspoon,
In the circle of them, many persons exchange
        small tokens,
They are that who cannot speak as I
        but send him forth alone
        uttering "I."

DEAR M.,

A good time, a basket load of refugees, a long canyon of washed vanity. All you want is what I ask. Wishing you could feel as I the principle of discretion he violated in the matter of funding you handled so vividly. He to me looked calmly beyond. Glad also to have spoken in terms of the relentless sign, my sundering by it, your long flight of stairs, stares, stars. I have been looking over what I have said and I have found that. Your little downstairs room with red phone, our happy meal over that shrink's son's poetry anxiety: we could have helped, alas! The little parcel of books you encouraged me to buy against my better wishes.

B. currently visiting, looking at the walls; R. trying not to remove her clothing; B. (another B.) slightly flirtatious; much talk of you involving pictures on the wall and reading one's inner acoustics. Is language perfect, and why can't we make sense of it once and for all? That is, the Martians already own some of our larger hotels. This is the last political statement they will allow me to make.

The book on N. is every bit as good as I was afraid it was (at that price!), especially the chapter on the "Beerhall Effect." The other books are in a pile waiting for next spring's thaw, your visit in January, the opening of a bordeaux from Bandol, which is difficult. The rest of the time was spent returning. Like the wine, it is open and formal. What you have taught me I am putting it to use. Watch me shake my knee under the table. I don't feel bad about your tendency to use my words, "knee," "jackanapes," "flirtatious" (a purple blouse and green pants), "tensions," and "language," the rest of which are yours for keeps.

Letters should be as intimate as money. That is, they should have a particular smell and texture that intimates their earlier lives. The ones I have sent you are still sitting here in a pile, and I often read them to underscore my sense of confusion. Here's one I thought you would like, had you received it:

Dear M., I anticipate a short visit to your area and would like to be put up with. Do you think you can share some toothpaste, naked urban vistas with saxophone, your wife, and charming child? Good, I will write you explaining the particulars. R. will go to the wrong airport, wait an hour, phone K. and realize his mistake. Chagrin will carry him to me as though on the wings of one of your lyrics (the one with the blue pencils). The rest of the letter will involve the framing of my apologies for rude remarks made under duress of rhetoric. Forgive me, they were made possible by your willingness to listen. Love, M.

Soon thereafter I will write you, feeling the vacuity of my six years' departure and imagine what experiences you failed to provide or inaugurate in my absence. This way, no one gets hurt and the policy goes to my starving wife who could use it. Always glad to help, raise little expectations in the sun. This is the start of winter, and sex is on the move.

Love,

    M.

RECONSTRUCTION

Since when was the refrigerator empty?
How many times do you work at the factory
during the past ten years?
I am a student, but have hunger,

and the starlings swirl themselves
around the plaza and sing
while Generalissimo is a tree-lined boulevard
in any city;

Hemingway etched his name
on the wall at El Candil,
and at night many of my friends
much divert themselves there;

we live on the third
above the Portuguese
who drive worse than the Madrileños
because now there are more cars;

at four in the morning
groups of the young
march under the window
clapping and singing;

Juan gives the book to him
who is his father,
the book is one I have read
when I used to read books;

in the afternoon we leaf
through the little yellow *Langenscheidt*
in search of eel or tripe
and the phrase how do I fix

the four-wheel-drive vehicle
with the verb for comprehend,
with a doctor you are you
unless he is a friend of the family

and thus familiar, a priest
is a father who is also an industrialist,
at eight we go to the many houses
and play checkers,

eat smelt, eggs, peppers, squid,
and drink a tinted wine,
soon we will leave our habitations
and go to the south,

the cities are white there
and the people do not speak correctly,
it is very beautiful,
it is prohibited to sing.

PASSAGE

for Robert Duncan

1. Everything becomes FIRE

2. A FUSE forms in the eye where nature loves to hide

3. As in that PARVIS where they ate us, a garden

4. Willing FOUNTAIN of war, boats burning in the harbor

5. Above sleeping men who do the world's business, a SEAM in time opens

6. In that CIPHER of flames where we read cities

7. Dogs bark at strangers but in the ASH all are one

8. SHADOW, picking rinds out of garbage

9. Midden from whose "He" and "She" they MESH

10. In these dark PASSAGES, courts of dreaming men

11. The stuff of the PSYCHE is a smoke-like substance of finest particles

12. Rising as a MIST from things that are wet

13. Morning field webs, yellow acacia, moist LEXIS

14. From heaps of rotting carcasses bring poppies of forgetfulness, a SWARM

15. Of bees like FLAMES rising

16. In the shuddering hives, a fluent GNOSIS, death's golden code.

II

1. Everything becomes water, a SWARM muttering

2. As though a SEAM ran through sound

3. Like a river of money and merchandise, a FIRE

4. Of exchange while in the PARVIS they intone an alphabet

5. From whose delta all CIPHERS are sound

6. Hudor, Thumon, Thalassa, MESH of fish and poison

7. As the bee dance maps a floral GNOSIS out of air

8. But men have not heard it though its FUSE is in the heart

9. LEXIS of contentions, first rime

10. And Dionysus, through whom they FLAME and speak in tongues

11. Is the SHADOW of Hades, Lord of the Dead

12. Their tongues are FOUNTAINS, their breath

13. Our moth, PSYCHE, hungering for light

14. Awake we see a dying world, asleep PASSAGES

15. The ASH keeps breath and death

16. As a MIST falling out of night.

DEAR M.,

Thus am I having back you are my friend. You noticed I didn't write nor speak loudly enough can you hear? This crisis certainly involves all of the reading you can take, but it exhausts me by its bigness. Lately I have been planting when in my spare time I am not work-ing. I have been listening as well, but the things are so difficult to exist by that I grow tired and then sleep. Once or twice I went to see what was playing, and they let me in. I felt deep gratitude but have forgotten what it was I saw. Oh, yes, there was a large pepper tree next to a river and elsewhere a pond. These images remind me of you, my old friend, because I am writing these down instead of forgetting them where they will do no one any good. The hedge is moving a little now; it's the wind, which this time of year comes in off the sea, I remember it all. It is good that you have been able to travel; there is so much to see and so little time. We must look very small from there who here appear so small. The twins, you see, did not really speak a separate language so much as one necessary in order to live in a town like that and with such parents. The film was made in three primary colors with several secondary ones to give it the flavor of reality. It is hard to know what they are driving at most of the time, our leaders, but they have a difficult job to do and do it to us in the best of our interests. Perhaps having power is like hav-ing images. This I what I saw when I fell asleep, a man trying to break down the door.

Love,

M.

In one the world was better

when they did it on the ground

with rocks and horns,

in the other the world will be better

when they learn to seize

the right lever,

in a mirror

a man is learning to sign

a phrase for I am speaking

MY FRENCH

A swan falls off the park bench
where it perches
to watch me swim, a cave
yawns beneath my ribs

because its toiling silver workers
have nothing left to mine,
boats only ride the horizon
on Thursday (at last,

the entertainment calendar!)
as though to illustrate
a distance not unlike the size
of this page; I speak

in the tongues of Taylor and Bradstreet
their tangled references to me
demand it, thus am I punished
for wanting appurtenances

a fissure, for example, that runs
through the fine print,
we can't read it
it runs through water.

"LITTLE CELLS, ORATORIES,
AND SEPULCHRAL RECESSES"

He learns to live with so much time
the world flattens into room and door
because five minutes walks around the block
to post an ardor made of back and thigh
as though the clock were made of mouth
breathing what were never vowels but skin
he sees through, listens to some surging
out beyond the cliff and comes to know
as mind (as mine), but red moon rises
over reefs he broke his ear on
now some occasion drives a phrase
beyond the papers, pots, and dinner leavings,
mountains fill the night with glacial carvings
muted cries, the phrase is very long
and full of wind, it's big enough
to fit in eyes as eyes between which
"and" and "and."

He must be in trouble
he can't go into the drugstore alone
they don't make drugstores anymore
and he is afraid of flying

because of something he ate
or was brought up to emulate
but they nurse him back to health
and he marries a registered nurse

who has learned to deal with snakes
and narrow stairways, a home
of their own is desirable
but difficult to pronounce: homo

erectus, which when they stand
complete whole sentences
like a man is being beaten
and man bites dog.

The Landing
of Rochambeau

1985

THE DREAM DREAM

I am in the book
(or "book")
I see my name
answering back

I am in a building
with stalls
I fall asleep
in the book

each stall sells
a different cure
the doors are locked
which is a cure

I am in "her" house
but these are "my" friends
the ramps and stairs
are steep

he offers to open the doors
for a price
I am outraged
I am eighteen

and riding a plane
made of glass
the books rise
to the ceiling

there is (are)
a man (men)
chasing me
with pincers

I am twenty-one
and riding a plane
and someone named "me"
gives me

my name, my name
is hers
she is twenty-one
or eighteen

depending on the boat
(or book)
or the name for you
that is very small

and hard to spell
or why I need
to read it
I am late for the boat

but it will wait
it is not a boat
but a wake.

THE WORDS ARE TRAPPED IN DOXA

Thin smoke rises from them
from the blue row houses on Walter Giesekingstrasse
next to the park
                or where you are not
thinking of anything and they throw you a ball

you have a choice: to throw it back
to throw it to a third or leave it lie
you can marry the tycoon's daughter
and perpetuate a sexual accident
or make a deal with the CIA
                          these are choices
no one makes for you and to have them
is to be alive
                but confused, how
cool it became on the patio, bugs
banging against the screen, a distant skunk
wafting over suburbia
                      I hear your nervous typewriter
because, nervous, I can't be alone
and they (bugs) want to get out
where the dark meets them (hello)
since they are dark and composing something
                              we are

not understanding
                    blue fish, green flash, happy tourist
school of low-cruising pelicans, flotilla
of ponderous seaplanes or a tree
of finches cheeping while the cat
lies at its base
                    "so many bites!"

it's summer, why move
thus close eyes and stretch, words
stretch with you

the people walk about the beach
and know nothing, but they talk
we know this because their mouths move
which also kiss and suck air
                    from a distance
the distance is close
                    they write letters
to seal it.

PAGE OF CUPS

for Helen Adam

Who would have known he had no hair
he had no clothes no shovel
no box to put it in no window
he carried from town to town
no ball to roll no eyes no mouth
pulled down at the edges in scorn
no factor no blood the tide was in
a moon thin behind thin clouds
the tools were gone no wonder
no rungs to the ladder no loft
to climb to here is his pencil
and here a flounder, a flat fish
without water no candle no needle
he knits with he knits with
to cover old mother no clock
makes him late here is his finger
pointing at rabbit at gander
here is his inside no bells
no anger when moon slides down
below saucer of star net
no deck with his card but she turns it
and sends it he sees it he says it
first water then land then creatures

of aether then Egypt its rivers
the mountains of Persia no helmets
no cannon no sleep divides his dreams
of waking by cities the dawn as Anubis
turning in ocean gold in windows
his mantle of morning no witness
but arm held before him no landscape
no handle

THE LANDING OF ROCHAMBEAU

The Captain calls his crew to the deck,
we are landing, he says,
he doesn't know what to say next
so he adds, be back by noon me hearties,
they don't believe him
this is not *Kidnapped*
and he would never use the word "hearties"
besides, it is 1780, the harbor
is filled with sails,
and the postmark covers some of them.

The Captain has gone below to pack,
I have never landed before, he thinks,
what do I wear?
so he stands looking into the mirror,
am I Rochambeau
or is this the name of my ship
or have we arrived at last in the Port
of Rochambeau where we will strike a deal
with natives; then he remembers
it is 1780, the water is jade green.

The Captain is astonished to learn
that the colonies have defeated the British

because of a "Stamp Tax;" we have landed
too late, he mourns and looks out the window
to his right (our left), tall masts jut
into the Fragonard sky
against which USA 10¢ is branded forever;
he approves of the lettering and decides
not to go ashore after all
but writes a postcard home:

We have landed, the Captain writes,
but not very well; it is 1780, and they are rowing
out to meet us; it is impossible to tell
whether we are rowing or they are rowing
or who they might be; many sails fill
the harbor and the postmark is rolling toward us
from Brooklyn on the left (my right),
please advise: this is history, and I am
caught in it without a thing to wear;
if only my name were Napoleon.

As it is, my life takes up
only seven lines in *The Reader's Encyclopedia*
where it is clear that Washington and I
defeated Cornwallis at Yorktown
and with the French Fleet (which must explain
those sails!) forced "his" capitulation,

the entry leaves "his" a bit vague
to make the landing of Rochambeau
a surprise for both sides, including the reader's,
who notices the pink sky of Watteau.

I am the Captain of this letter, which begins
Dear Home, how I miss the Lisbon Earthquake
the Jansenist purges and leeks with egg,
remember Rochambeau in a foreign port
who must be content with corn and the inflated rhetoric
in pamphlets; I look up, he looks up
we regard him pausing midhistory
for a figure of speech like the ones he used to use
when writing Mme. R. in Potsdam
like you are the author of my heart.

But it is 1780, and the Captain never writes postcards,
after all, he is a man of action
and knows his fleet, the harbor
in which his ships lie at anchor,
he knows the sky, so common to USA
and the water, emerald blue,
I'll go ashore, he says, throwing down his pen
and have a drink avec mon equipage
dans les petites boites du port
I know at last what to wear.

For I am Jean Baptiste Donatien de Vimeur
le Comte de Rochambeau and I have landed,
the water is blood red with history,
and we are in its claws (he likes
the figure and writes it in his journal
then strides up to the deck
where the weather is clear)
"Lower the boats," he cries to a sailor,
"I will go ashore to the Bronx
where my name will be streets and parks."

But there is no sailor to hear him,
the deck is empty, and the postmark
covers most of the fleet;
it has turned cold since Rochambeau landed,
and when the French learn what USA 10¢ means
they will cut off his title, le Comte
no longer, only a name
in a time on a stamp on a card
for a reader who turns away from 1780
and remembers the water, white as their eyes.

IF TO WITNESS

If to witness is to persons unafraid or blank that is where a blue
line meets a convinced corner. If to judge by violins or a lozenge
the results be they of a mottled or variegated surface and distin-
guished by no less than three nor more than five contusions upon
the skin a confidence may be restored, the guests issued into the
cold night and you satisfactorily returned to your small rural home
with dog. Which is to say if to declare by canopy or other brightly
colored awning that a person of such-and-such a height wearing
green or gray plaid could exert him or herself in a way so as to ren-
der amazement, as it were, a foreign sentence dropped amid the
conversation and you off by train tomorrow for the north then
passing references to your person incomprehensible during the
evening and concerning the better part of one's capacity for writ-
ing in journals might attain that point or points wherein your
intention to speak coincides with their intention to hear, the
resulting uncomfortable silence being the only sign of such free-
dom that further conversation could only exacerbate an already
tense moment and remind you of a technical device something like
a microphone or perhaps a mushroom growing beside a fallen cedar
somewhere else.

JE SUIS IT

From the desperate city you go into the desperate country and have to console yourself with the bravery of minks and muskrats.
—THOREAU

He wanted a small circle
and a larger vantage
from which to see the village
while

members of his family
dropped off in his hands
a motor started of its own
accord

at least one sibling
in every household
was crazy, I
was once a child

and they extracted pennies
from my ears, see
how many wheels and gears
how many knives

in a clearing, a bare
common, he tries not

to walk into a tree
this is easier

than I thought, he thinks
and walks into a tree,
the readership is limited
to three aged librarians

and the janitor
who eats small boys,
let us consider what most
of the trouble and anxiety

is about and how necessary
that we be troubled
if to transcend the word is first
to leave the ground

if to pour is to be of that
which is poured
there must be a door and
behold, there is a door

solemnly he takes his hand,
castrati sing the anthem
for dead bicycles, blue
would be a good color

to paint the field
if it weren't for the numbers
on each blade, he
resolves to take the bus

and live alone on rice
to eat a turnip
in the spirit of adventure
and make a little stool

for the school nurse
in this way he grows beyond
the town pump, zinnias
tower over youth and youth

towers over something
indigestible, he hears
America calling
and goes in that direction.

ANSWERING MOTION

A mode he wants to master writes itself despite his intentions.
A mode he wants to witness writes him as master.

How to move through to answer the question, posing in its place
as that for which the question exists something otherwise quite
permanent.

Never interesting until allowed; once allowed interesting useless
as interesting.

How to solve the problem through the words, not by means of,
they so have their own formulations in the way you have your
discriminations.

The form allows it, not imposes itself, allows what never could be
expected and allows for that allowance including its refusal.

Not the problem to be solved so much as the problem to be pro-
posed without its being referred to.

To permit movement without end yet enjoying the illusion of
movement toward, enjoying the feel of it and its distractions.

There is something else.

When nothing is there and still having to go beyond that to the
things that start arguing against nothing.

Not to make it easier than it is, still he calls on an old formulation for advice and careens off in another direction.

As if to build around a manner of speaking without its terms and then to find that the terms were already in place.

To repeat as if.

Having something having a point and having a substance then having the time to know you have something again.

Paradox of making sense: you must have been an idiot not to have seen it before.

Wants to cover everything by illustration so comprehensive the illustration itself seems redundant.

Attention to this leads to attention to this; you can't not be here while searching for your coat.

Listening for what comes next having heard what came prior argues against nothing happening.

This much, if adequate, startles as being the somewhat less for which more asks.

THE EXEGETE

At the desk
      you have gone away
at home
      you invent things for me to say
in the pool
      you play chess
      and I watch from above
in the door
      you are halfway here
in the window
      there is a window
      plus a face
at the crossroads
      you are wearing a sign
writing and what it is not
      make a sound in the desert
you are a five-pointed star
      given as a present
the sound of someone waiting
      for an answer
      a small hand with narrow fingers
this line means endless life
      this one means you grow older
in the mountains

you come to a narrow pass
clinging for dear life
    you are asked to perform
    a dangerous operation
on the streets
    you put your arm around her
broken portions of the song
    run through your head
    attached to an image
in the crowd
    there is a crowd
    of persons around her
where you are
    someone has just turned away
turned a corner in the script
    where the reader has learned
    how to read
in the margins
    a tiny note:

    continue: don't continue

THE REPORT

It's beautiful, but I don't think I like it
or it's appropriate but unnecessary,
the dog likes it, takes it into her little house
where it releases its effect
like a paperweight releasing its snow,
and the report lists everything
the gunfire
the sound of the gunfire
the reports of the sound of the
bodies falling, their earrings left in a drawer
to be found later by a relative,
these accumulate and in time
become the book of the best intentions
which the report incorporates
among the interviews with dead children
and the aesthetics of a perfect object

READY TO HAND

Take the case of another
and I take it
it feels like ochre, a middle
in which a memo

is written, black crows
perch on the ledge
a small man below
becomes an object

and I seize it, it
comes off in my hands
like a handle
where there had been an intention

not to hurt
but to effect change
I wrote out the words
as though placing my hands

on a throat
it felt soft
and the blood was familiar
like middle C

where it lodges in fingers
not ominously
this is only one example
there are others.

MORE IS UP

He works hard

        A man breaks rocks with his bare hands

I hope it works out

        Standing before the mirror he regards the
        body lifting weights as my own

She made a big mistake

        She can tell that the dough has risen by the
        sound of exploding lightbulbs

We should be on time

        He stands on his watch tapping his foot
        while she reads a map

I will reach my goal

        I already understand the padlock

I am in school

        Is easier to say than I am during school

That happens in life

        When two trains going in opposite direc-
        tions pass, sometimes a man walking toward
        the rear of the car appears to be standing still

She is excellent in her field

                  She is buried up to her neck, but her voice is
                  admired by the forest creatures

He will rise to the top

                  A man follows his bubbles

She set her goal

                  Pouring the concrete first and then adding
                  the wicket brought the crowd to their feet

We will reach our aim

                  Is hard to do with only two arms

He put it in words

                  First he pounded it senseless with a mallet

I disagree with Plato when
he says that

                  He was around here a minute ago

We have a small problem

                  But then we are very small

Your meaning is clear

                  I can see straight through you

You must understand it
in context

                In their country the steering wheel
                is on the right side in order to
                accommodate their tollbooths

They have a good inter-
personal relationship

                Anything else would be obscene

I determine it
on my scale of success

                In the left-hand dish I put a list of
                my achievements; in the right I
                place my fist

This is common
in the world

                He placed a potato between two
                facing mirrors

THE MEMO

Nous aurons écrit sur la surface ondoyante d'un souffle!
—EDMOND JABÈS

We might read from the book on private language
or we might speak a private language
made up of doubt
plus the sounds of a child

imitating the family parrot:
he is green
he is going to the toilet
how do you say how do you say

we have papers from the government
and collections of secrets
one of them goes like this:
a man has offended another

not by anything said
but by a tone in which what is said
is returned, made
perfectly clear

so that after the conversation
the second man conceives a diabolical plot

in which a man may be marked
by his falseness

and so may be mistrusted in his lonely way
among the also-marked,
he has indicated his plot
in a memo to the world

but has coded his intentions
in the bland diction of an institution
that has provided him with paper
and soft lead pencils,

in his neighborhood
before the mockingbirds have begun their racket
someone's lost parrot flies across a metallic sky
calling to a space he was not permitted to know

with the vocables of an intelligent child
just beginning to hear difference,
a man wakes to hear it
and resolves never to make war on humans

which becomes the first line of his dream
as he falls back to sleep.

Analogy
of the Ion

1987

ANALOGY OF THE ION

for David Bromige

*If the world, instead of being beauty, were nothing but equally large
unvariegated boulders, there would still be no repetition.*
—KIERKEGAARD

I

There would be a first word and it would permit the first one to
speak it.

It's hard not liking a philosophy made out of chairs and slabs
the force of an idea becoming gradually a sentence and later you
meet for lunch.

They arrive at the Brick Hut as an afterthought the airport
was closed because of a quake he barely got off the ground is it
the food or the name he prefers?

Following writing a faint ghost in green of what he said for a
brief moment fills the screen and then dies.

Up there in Sonoma, down in L.A., back in the Midwest, out
in Wyoming she studies the law where jurisdiction does not
occur in the same place twice.

What will he say according to the rules you show interest in
the other person's not having paid any particular attention and
with such enthusiasm.

The circle is the house is the measure is the map is the sky.

Paper wraps stone, stone flattens scissors, scissors cut paper
you could also write them and achieve the same effect.

He achieved a materiality that only metaphysics could explain.

They became friends of mimesis, each referring to himself by the other's name.

He wrote out of a desire to stand over history, one foot in the Adriatic and the other in the Lago di Garda, while soldiers made their way up treacherous mountains of typographical errors and false etymologies.

Other news included how to wave at the judges.

To distinguish between the penis and the phallus he wrote his father's name in his notebook and then tore out the page.

By gradually gathering parts of various board games from thrift shops he created new objects out of vestigial commands no longer linked to the tiny swans and barns and cups that had been their actors.

In the north in the south in the west in the east there was still the position of in.

The opinion spoke of the failure of the arrangement to achieve intrinsic and continuing reality.

But we exist in the belief that toothpaste and mayonnaise shall never occur in the same sentence.

It was a familiar story the lover seeks to be comforted nothing will suffice maybe by singing someone will hear him the autumn winds blow the leaves over his guitar, etc.

The earthquake had served warning that next time it would take out Glendale and half of the Burbank airport.

They had contrived a solution to the problem of the homeless by reinterpreting their plight as a need to assert their freedom to chose not to come indoors.

He hankered after a good hamburger.

You can erase these mistakes with ease became you can erase these mistakes with ease.

Each morning the city unrolled its plan slowly from the hills down to the bay as the fog lifted and the neighbors opened their windows.

Epos is not cold history he wrote slash he writes.

And behold our dynasty came in between an oil shortage and an oil glut this will be recorded somewhere.

Had he been wasting his time making empty statements of fact was the only way he could frame his discomfiture over the absence of interrogatives.

The grid falls apart where S meets A, but it is also the oldest intersection in town.

II

The brochure defines the project but what does a project define?

The sound of its (a city of indeterminate size, aspirations, or tax base) conveyances drowns out the harpsichord.

After which he could reflect on a certain dynastic calm that came with his pension.

One of the projects involved cutting down a tree to make way for a magnetic recording center, the tree plated with steel and replanted with a tiny speaker that plays country-western songs.

After all it was a replaceable culture and so long as you avoided reference to the structure anything could be said for the first time.

You think of all of the relevant cases in which thinking is possible (on the spot, in reflection, out loud) and imagine the same object.

He puts a bag over his head and counts to an unimaginable number.

He first conceived the world as a shape discovered in the Oz books and later as a geometrical theorem it was empty and could contain anything.

You could imagine a world that begins once they cross the Red Sea or else one that mimics the Diaspora itself, but scientists now believed that the waters parted by natural causes so another world was born that incorporated the previous two.

Another project involved a series of Stonehenge-like pilings that had become a popular place for the chancellor to have his picnics.

His marginal comments were gender neutral, but she wondered when a pen was not a pen.

Defectors were signing their decisions in carefully worded statements leaked to the press the implication was that power had been handled badly they included pictures.

He liked the idea of photographs better than the actual products and justified his distaste by reading some of the recent literature.

What he meant by A at that early date was not what he meant, now he was at pains to point out in a series of published disclaimers.

So far their new vantage had been framed by the great oak worm disaster that even if it didn't kill the trees left a great deal of their structure exposed for future generations.

He had been mentioned in an oblique context and because it was phrased badly felt obliged to dissociate himself if not from the sentiment at least from its grammar.

Up here, up there, up ahead, up north, there remains the position of down.

A code violation was being repaired by a man in the back of the house listening to the hearings while in the front another listened to the Beatles she couldn't compute.

A critic so famous that his review had forced Satie to confront him physically on the Pont Neuf.

Only the measure of squirrels running across the roof controls the deployment of his phrases.

A history is also a story the word is unambiguous on this point.

III

If plus heat
three as three
a man marked man
is inconclusive
and woman swims
simply open
then comes France
an immobile
and pertinent thus
returns through water
harp and flute and heat
bends horizon from
they don't answer
a pervasive clear
I took this picture
ample bay glass
or pinched vantage
the sign warms
through slippage very
soprano ice column
he writes at desk
the Denver Tosca
up here out there
was patient even

birds on deck
I quit
large columnar columns
as if water could
ice tray
four impresses nine
called bleeding winces
he so
and makes small talk
a cogent article
plus four plus extra
leaf damage but
the illusion of shattering
arresting heat
thanks I'll not
and behold novelty
progress keeps lever
this last.

IV

SOKRATES: Hail Ion, enviable rhapsode wherefrom are you come?

ION: From Epidaurus where I won another contest.

SOKRATES: You know I envy you reciters always well dressed and
hanging out with poets, especially Homer whose lines
are nice but whose thought's sublime.

ION: True enough, not to know Homer is not to know.

SOKRATES: Will you embellish him in our purview awhile?

ION: Indeed crowns trumpets laurels annointments fall on
           my head you've come to the right place.

SOKRATES: Now I'm just a dumb hick, hardly worth talking to,
           but answer me one thing: Don't all poets say the same
           thing? Why Homer and not, say, Hesiod?

ION: I can't figure it out. When others mention others I
           frankly doze but Homer wakes me, explain this riddle.

SOKRATES: No problem. First it's not from knowing that comes
           your knowledge of Homer but from a power divine.
           What you say is not what you say but what is said
           through you, agreed?

ION: You've got the floor.

SOKRATES: A poet is a light and winged thing, never composed
           until he's drunk a draught and then he soars. It's not by
           art he sings of arms and men but by that chain he
           shares with one he'd heard somewhere before. And like
           a chain you too are linked to Homer just as some are
           linked to Orpheus and others to Musaeus, and when
           the light foot hears you you either dance or doze.

ION: And so we reciters read the readers, if I read you right.

SOKRATES: Right, I figured you'd come round. But wait. Let's say
           you're saying some Homer one Tuesday, and you come
           to the part where Odysseus unmasks himself before the
           suitors, you know the part?

128

ION: I'm all mouth.

SOKRATES: Or where Achilles rushes Hektor aren't you trans-
           ported, aren't you an action?

ION: I'm hardly in the room. My hair stands up, my heart's
           in another planet.

SOKRATES: So there's your audience, eyes brimming; they ache
           because you ache. Man thinks he lives by art alone but
           muses tend to trickle down their inspiration you but
           breathe through. And your audience is the final link in
           that great chain the muses sing as if to say, "we hope
           you like our song. Liking's not our concern but yours."
           In short you're not the speaker but the spoke.

ION: Well put, but you can't tell me that though I'm mad
           when reading Homer I can't praise in him the things I
           know.

SOKRATES: On which point?

ION: On every point without exception.

SOKRATES: Even on those points upon which you have no knowl-
           edge?

ION: And what matters might those be?

SOKRATES: Chariots, for example. What are those lines where
           Nestor speaks to Antilochus, his son, warning him
           about the turning post in the race in honor of
           Patroclus? I'll recite them, if you like.

ION: No, give me the reins where I own the car:
           At the post lean left

of the rest

then goad the off horse

with hand

give him free rein

and at the turn

let near horse come close

enough to graze the stone

but don't hit it.

SOKRATES: Very good. Now on the matter of chariots whom do
you trust, Homer or Horser?

ION: Horser no doubt.

SOKRATES: Because who better to know the art of horse than he
who rides? Homer's but a lexicon of horsey things, but
only those who ride know how to hold the reins. In
other words each art speaks whereof it knows, do you
not agree?

ION: I admit of differences among things which separately I
know not.

SOKRATES: Precisely, for in many poems we take for granted what
we're given, yet admitting differences we can't adjudi-
cate at all. So if the rhapsode knows not the art of spin-
ner, charioteer, or general yet speaks of spinning, riding,
and leading troops how can he claim to speak on their
behalf. Or better put, what does a rhapsode know?

ION: Well, a rhapsode knows the kind of speech a general
makes or a woman the kind of wash she describes
we're talking power over diction here.

SOKRATES: And having power over diction is having power over
women and animals?

ION: Unquestionably, I say with trepidation, Sokrates.

SOKRATES: So whoever is a rhapsode is also an able general.

ION: They're both a single.

SOKRATES: And thus a general is also a rhapsode by such logic?

ION: Nope, it doesn't work the other way around.

SOKRATES: Why not? You are the most able rhapsode in Greece
and the ablest general as well?

ION: You said it, not me. What can I say, I learned it all from
Homer.

SOKRATES: So we Athenians should hire you, knowing all you
know not only of Homer but of general things.

ION: I'd take the job.

SOKRATES: But (and here's the catch) if you know by art what you
couldn't possibly know by craft are you not like
Proteus simply art twisted round a likelihood? And if
you, as you say, speak winged words without the
benefit of reason how can you in honesty speak these
praising words of Homer? Choose, therefore, how you
will be called by us a man unjust or a man divine?

ION: Simple: to be divine is just.

SOKRATES: And a lovelier title it is, Ion, to be divine in simple
mindedness than be artful in praising Homer.

V

In other dialogues I've argued that poets corrupt the morality of the State, but here, for the sake of argument, I claim that the only good poet is one who knows what he's talking about. Ion may be a good reciter of Homer, but he doesn't know from poetry—precisely because there's nothing there to know. Poetry is a cipher of everything everyone has said already and to repeat it is only to validate this very fact. To analogize, however, is to have your Ion and your dialogue too. As I said somewhere in the Gorgias, speaking of rhetoric, these arts have no subject but themselves; they feed on other arts but have at their center only words. To propose that poetry involves knowledge is rank folly and is why poets should leave theory to those with academic positions or at least a federal grant. With these credentials one can dissolve categories, split hairs and contradict oneself at will. Although it has gotten a bad name in recent years, Science offers the critic the very authority he needs to assert these truths and to do so without having to get his hands muddy at the public trough of so-called popular opinion. He can rise above the contentions of ordinary dialectics by pointing to the flaws in vulgar speech, all the while claiming solidarity with those unfortunates who use it. Ion loses the argument every time by his inability to apply such authority to an art that more properly belongs to translators: since they can't produce anything of their own, they merely reproduce what others give them. Ion thinks that to know how to read is to know what one reads when in fact he is unread by his own assertions. I believe in a separation of church and state, so to speak: the man who believes and the man who thinks are one centaur, and no association of sensibility will be of much use except to the makers of mirrors. It is worth upholding the distinction between art and life because in so doing you get to buy shares in both. Which is precisely why, although I've been known to stand behind the arras and listen to Ion do his rendition of Penelope at the well, I must publicly renounce the watery words he uses. Language is all superstructure; it can't do anything of its own, which is why I have made such a profession of professing nothing. At least in this way, when the revolution comes, I won't be stuck with hemlock as my only recourse. Who knows, I might be made secretary of defense for my aptitude at manipulating a press conference.

VI

Then fog minus hills
four as before or
woman marked man
speech without word and
one speaks
hardly closed
because from Greece
a protean wind
but irrelevant nor
advances skirting shores

piano and drum and
refracting vicinity by
because they don't hear
a partial static
while you stood there
limited inlet mirror
either expansive focus
the sign cools
by tension hardly
baritone mist arras
she fingers knife
the Dallas Norma
out there up here
will approach odd
absence of birds in
you begin
miniscule redundant globes
but ice might
fire pan
five is impartial to
sent coagulate I smile
she that
but elaborates
the independent article
minus nine minus less
leaf damage and

the fact that coherence

releases wind

recrimination he'd better

but ignores repetition

repetition loses to button

that first.

VII

It means the same this writing so why write?

Yet he attempts to dissolve a complex web by referring to the trees from which it hangs.

A tree is a complex web in whose branches live creatures who emerge in the crepuscular hours to look upon us with dark eyes.

They met not to consolidate a position but to consume a possible hamburger.

In between the first and second descriptions a tense had changed even though both refer to the same event.

He refuses to admit the object as in any way determining the shape of sound a flute makes reaches his ear and continues to the other side.

The speechwriter was fired for having implied that the candidate was not the origin of his speech.

The dialogue would never have occurred if the heat had not forced the two friends out into the country where they heard the chirping of the cicadas.

Having spoken only to the other's answering machine for several days he was surprised to encounter the actual voice of his friend and promptly hung up.

They imagine that stories have their origin in action but we who have heard no such stories must simply interpret the language of birds.

They showed us the photograph of the miniature city modeled on the actual city in which they had stayed, which included a perfect replica of the miniature city within the miniature city and so forth.

And Thoth came to him and exhibited his various arts, which included drafts and dice as well as writing, and said that this discipline my king will make the Egyptians wiser and will improve their memories.

He is unclear whether the first time he saw his father was in the living room or in the photograph of the living room in which his father appeared in uniform.

Only a spoken word can have a father, hence he is one of the logoi, one who argues.

Once the four great stones with the Greek word for "wave" roughly etched in each were put in place the students followed suit by carving their own names into the surface.

Once it was new and then it became time.

VIII

Back then, recently, not so long ago, once upon a time he wrote.

In other words, no theory can be produced without considering the making of me, myself, and I.

He heard persons walking past his closed car as leaves rustling in the wind.

"I made her so mad she was burning" caused her to underline "she was burning" she was so mad.

He achieved a metaphysics that only materialism could contain.

An earlier judge had been easily confirmed but he, unlike the current candidate, had had the good sense not to write his opinions in a material form.

A tree-like grid imposed itself on the actual tree, allowing him to understand an architecture the leaves obscure.

A tree like God impressed itself unnatural tree she saw the towers the leaves obscure she read and in them cast adrift alternate measures the dance.

Her greatest pleasure before discovering Paris had been diagramming sentences oddly enough.

Our age came in because of a vast displacement.

Achieving mastery implied having read the book prior to discussing it, though many gained theirs by assuming others hadn't and opening their mouths.

In the interim between one section and the next the caterpil-
lars had turned into moths and now flitted brightly among skele-
tal branches.

In paradise solitude is painful to a social mind.

The letters contained references to persons now scattered
about the landscape who are at this point and by displacement
largely textual and from henceforth will be known as A, B, C, et
cetera.

I miss the typewriter the cautious approach to the right margin
tail on the letter q, western vistas in the logo of Remington bell.

Memory was invented somewhere back in the eighteenth
century but you wouldn't know it.

Many of the missing details could be obtained by phoning
the individuals in question who invariably contradicted what
others had said earlier history is a perpetual phone call.

He was a partisan of many Gallic systems.

The famous critic was on his way to deliver a speech on desire
when he met a Dante scholar on a bridge, words were exchanged,
they came to blows, he arrived to his lecture late with a black eye.

Light had taken on new meaning now that conifers and oaks
had replaced sage and mustard though eucalyptus is ubiquitous in
both places causing neighbors much uneasiness.

He wrote out of a desire to stand in the midst of history like
a tall tree with the great spirit blowing through him on its way to
the present.

Do you mind if I share your table?

Poetry lifts the veil from the hidden beauty of the world and makes familiar objects be as if they were not familiar.

Death is a condition, not a promise.

FROM

Post Hoc

1990

POST HOC

When the bell rings twelve times
the grid begins; at the end of the grid
a punctuation and before long
action becomes possible

the word for action is delay
this way a point bleeds into the fabric
until it is revealed as a face
and the name of the face

will bring people to the fence
when a picture bleeds
he is not in time but time
is what you call it

then they will bring you money
and the bell has done its office
the body
permits you to leave the body

FOOTNOTE

and if there is a grid
there must have been depth
if he becomes lost in a forest
there must be streets in the town

and objects in windows
that alert the shopper
to a power
he can never equal

hence to be flat
is to repeat flatness
against which the moat
the maiden and the apparition

stand in relief, the tale
can be used later
to illustrate the ill effects
of theft

SONNET

One who speaks of the multifariousness of voices
one through whom the voices speak speaks twice
once through rapt inflections breath on fire
once as metal fathers rising in the blood
the voice becoming wire and things said through it
thinner still so that
one who standing on the outside of a logos looking in
is one who sits within and reaching for the phone
arrives at speech his own by way of voices
he but replicates and theirs ventriloquized in him
are later written down: tundra, reindeer
permafrost that lives beneath the breath
all spring partly vocable and partly simply cold;
the witness is unspeakable someone dead
who speaks the name a footstep leaves ahead

SUBJECT MATTER (A REWRITE)

I'm afloat on a sea, see,
and this sloop comes into view
that could be a seal
or a green furl of a wave

but it's not
it's a numeral
and there's this naked guy   and there's this naked person
who's not wearing any—   it illustrates

thing you could put your hand on
trying to illustrate a dream   whose name must be "Fig."
first you open the door   a frame to modify a door
and it's the wrong room   like a way of walking
                                    around a reservoir

you've been there before
then you climb a flight
and someone stares at you   filling in a form
this much is familiar   with questions framed around it
                                    like where do you begin

stars form a story overhead   and instantly there are all these
cities made out of
minor metropolises   stairs you could climb
and you are caught in it   or where to end, say

trying to catch a bus
for which there is no change
chance never enters into it
some parts of speech
and a fourth
I'm hardly necessary

to keep up appearances
but still I compose
red for the "ideal string"
black for the "concrete anchors"

gold
for where a ship falls
into a book whose name

is what the sea saw

it must have been me

in Tasmania at the horizon
in the furled leaves of a coleus

a life force minus the life
equals number, one
two sentences dis-
cover a third city
in whose multiple talk
something like talk occurs

it is late spring
fog forms in the afternoon
I listen to you in Arcadia
where the light is gold

and in multiple strings

you become a voice
it must have been mine saying
ancient gong, ancient song

sing of land's end
when you see two skies
one of eyes
the other of seas

MIXED ARYAN

The parochial blessings of an all-too-familiar ethnicity
Call to mind our youth in Winsor Parish
Which returns this windy night as a dream of parents
Who speak on the subject of our neighborhoods or the separation
Of prose and verse it hardly matters you are a white boy
In a green world power is held by the few we are enslaved
And so forth you pick up the theme from the genes
And submit it as your civics project in fifth period
For which you get a C from Mrs. Callous
But what did you expect
She's a teacher and probably a member of the Party
As they told you at the American Legion convention
Later you work for the Weenie King
And learn what goes on in Fairy Land
Radicalization comes slow among the painfully self-conscious
Where to see a tree is to become the wind
Or the music it calls to mind to see it with
It's hard to regard a tree as a commodity
But you learn and there are others handing you books
Covertly at first and then in broad daylight,
As your color changes the tax base remains the same
Soon you are almost Italian, then French, whole vistas
Of the underprivileged are revealed in the pages of Max Weber
Which is very black and white

And soon these tropes have come full circle
To enclose you as the wind last night kept you awake
Only to heighten what the darkness gave you back, if fitfully,
And which continues in another form
Though you will seem to have invented it yourself
And this, too, is a blessing.

THE SECOND CITY

for Cathy Simon

Even though there are motorized conveyances
I am on foot; even though there is a map
I negotiate the streets by landmark

there are no landmarks
but a series of edges
common to several cities

the hill is in San Francisco,
the great shopping district
with its glittering windows

and esplanade before the fountain
is in New York
and the river with its bridges is in Paris

I'm working on the park
with its glass botanical gardens
marble pillars in the distance

leftover from the exposition
there is probably a hill
from which I descend

and arrive at the "market district" below
clearly indicated by the word "brick"
like those on the west side of Buffalo

to make this descent
is to parse the terrifying grid
of hill cities, roads

dead-ending against canyons, barriers
where a street careens into space
and continues below

bearing the same name
so that a second city rises
out of the forgotten one

more pointed because not yet filled in
by monument or palisade
the place where water touches land

and forms a line
the leaflike veins of streets
it is too late

for the bus
and I must walk from North Beach
to the Bronx or something with a *B*

through the middle city
the place a middle occupies
when you are no longer familiar

and the buildings have only been seen
by night from a car
and by lights

I am afraid
someone will address me in French
and I will forget the word for myself

having so recently arrived
and yet to be a stranger
is to be swallowed up

without words
without glasses
bearing an envelope with a numbered series

in the second city
I live out the dream of the first
living neither for its access and glamour

nor dying from its disregard
simply talking toward the twin spires
of an ancient cathedral
like a person becoming like a person

THINKING THE ALPS

It was by just such a state of logical perpendiculars
that "Bob" had arrived at this narrow pass
in the mountainous netherworld between being and time
and was preparing to reconnoiter the future
according to a long-descending trope
of seven or eight partial figures complete with suffixes
until he arrived at the minimal camp below
its cookstove and portable toilet.

How had he come to this fork in what was up to now
a cliché-ridden pursuit of normalcy with an unparalleled view
of deviance spreading out like conifers on either flank
their prepositions exfoliating according to a Persian design
the rug of which you see in Figure 3
where "Bob" decries a motif not unlike himself
as gatherer of leeches the better to invent
the trail that up to now he'd thought went straight ahead

but which appears to tarry, disappear, and die
in sedgy grass among scattered tarns where to continue
is to be lost in an ancient folio illuminated by monks
parsing miracles in canons first intoned
on the one true cross, and "Bob" is but a ghostly sign
of a polluted cleft between Europe and Asia through which

Satan's armies drive a fetish plus handmaidens
into Paris just in time for Mardi Gras.

Suddenly vertical time bisects his gaze
suggesting action as a cure for vertiginous thought
and "Bob" moves forward pulling Melancholy, his burro, behind
hearing all the time the crowd's cascading cheers
from every canyon wall as he concludes the Brückner Fourth
mopping his brow and making his way to the concertmaster
to shake a hand still vibrating from an undiminished chromaticism
in the works since Tartini's *Devil's Trill*.

It's hard walking while conducting conversations
among ourselves thinks "Bob," yet where would we be
when faced with an actual business lunch composed of hands
holding knives and forks, their corporate bonhomie
reflected in certain iambics he imitates, voices
heard in falling water, crowds at airports, even these lines
must be saying something if we can stop them long enough
for a path to declare itself among infernal shades of type.

I'm not just anyone caught in a parable, he boasts
for all the good it does him, product of the culture
that needs examples of aspiring men to build its cars from
still everyone needs a logo and I'm as good
as Andrew Carnegie on a stamp and better equipped

to be canceled at post offices by the sea
in which a postmaster has a taste for Cherubini
which he plays to salve the patience of the lines that form

reminding "Bob" of action whereupon he shifts his pack
and takes his first step since stanza four
destroying the Lake Poets in the process
while history breathes a sigh of relief and the owl
of Minerva takes flight, French horns in unison
strike up the autumnal largo from a woody glade
as workers go back to work, presses start up,
and DeQuincy renews his quest for the snowy shack of Kant

Crisp wind flutters through the latter half
of the Industrial Revolution as "Bob" becomes
a lathe, screw, and spinning jenny making life tough
on the workers but easy on capital
which is why he sings without end, erasing intervals
in a landscape he just might buy some day, but for now
he is alone in a wood, in the story of the wood
and its conclusion that lies just ahead through those trees

which are made of wood, design of the sepulcher already etched
in a frieze by Brancusi, which "Bob" hopes to inhabit
but that for now is memory thrown forward like the trail
he now concludes, drops his pack and stirs the coals

the better to become an ad for coffee
I'm almost up to modernism he thinks, and yet this solitude
prohibits me from being here, if only Melancholy faithful guide
could talk he'd make this ruined camp a home.

Holding steaming cup aloft he compares those cliffs
so recently declined to one of either sex
in whose airy gaze one sees oneself (are all those mirrors mine
"Bob" asks, or has the Forest Service placed them here
that visages might animate the trees they hang on)
as if we could be a prelude to ourselves
but that's crazy he thinks and besides I need to eat
and saying so pours water into sawdust for a stew.

Sun sets over campsite, pines shimmer in the astral twilight
that chills the weary traveler
with reminders of where he's not, and slipping into his cocoon
after humping up the coals, "Bob" enters time
like a man stepping out of a long poem at the other end
and says good-night to faithful Melancholy chewing grass
and proceeds into that land his author never planned to enter
source of all descents that once begun beget another.

LORDS OVER FACT

I come to the letter eight
and start over
I come to the letter sixteen
it is the same thing

the same as one
done fifteen times
until the wings work by themselves
which is the letter two

and with this I take up the card
and write "two
never again to begin
for the first time"

and though I move steadily east
I continue the precession of four
doubled and redoubled
until I am almost not myself

so much a part of time
that number is only a tic
and old habit of one in its disguise
as three and its avatars

among leaves and the lame
and the trail so familiar
to the abject nineteen
unable to go on to twenty

he stands by the turnstile
at the sign of remainder
unlike zero the impossible one
partly the figure at the window

who has always gone and partly not
so that when you look out
it is six and seven, the letters
form a screen like prayer

that the ground might have something left
that water be allowed to stand
where it gathers in pools
nine

the sound of it roaring below the horizon
so that only dogs
know what is coming
they won't print this

because it is written by a dog
I speak for him

and translate eleven through fourteen
as quarters of the yard

ten is the forbidden zone
and even I draw a line around it
as it draws around me
something of its solitude

rain grows in the fold
between one layer
and the next
until stone is all they can say

so that to invoke the number five
is to begin life again
feet form around it
and stars become points

that only eighteen can destroy
anything more than itself
is excessive and necessary
ten plus seven plus

the one we will have forgotten to pack
the minus that opens a rock
the rock that carries a key
telling of old weather

the time before weather
when the letters began to coalesce
and one thing entered another
often quite alone

REWRITE

Once he had this face
and then he turned over
and had this other

"burned over 90 percent"
or simply getting older
of his body there were

faces yet to know
yet his own was not among them
he meant to say "one"

burning from within
a reaction to something he took
yet was actually getting older

and after all you burn
until there is no fuel left
you are left with a face

out of which you glare
others match theirs
to yours, it is

Once he had this face
and then turned over
and was another

had been burned
over 90 percent of his body
or else his skin

fell in sheets from bones
that made a face
his own, he meant to say

I burn from within
I speak from a face
I no longer have

but after all the skin
is "really there"
you have this face

and people address themselves
to your glance, it is
not yours

not enough yet once
in a dark mirror
you think at least mysterious

and walk back among them
waiting, and then the words begin
somewhat easier

but some words you think
to use against them
mostly friends

having skin also
where the mouth begins
the pain could not be described

CLOUD

It doesn't show
but I'm making up a new word
to replace Plato
with a tape delay

but that's two words
one for you and one
the first makes possible
impossible to say

in unison but in time
a cloud will return
in the same shape
and you call upon

an Ion to verify
an elephant but he'll say
anything
the power of suggestion

is water
he never forgets

ELSEWHERE

Over here in window
I prepare resolution once again
thin streams of water coat the glass
that visibility sets out to destroy

by turning on a light, slowly
I become solid
and without friends
in whose voices dispersal

is what they call me
not without affection
still
the names of those trees

slide away
so that almost a cube
I will a body into words
and talk like one

using rain as guide
all night it dropped on the roof
I left myself
to imagine

and then while the world
was still tipped on its end
he slid back into sleep
and the inner ear

was left to explain
how it was done, it was
not for me to know
as those shapes

(lozenge of yellow and white plane
green triangle
discerned through frosted glass)
are almost always moving

threading
the rectangle of vision
with a fable made mostly
of weather

one
you will lose yourself
two
become the opposite

three
carry the message

known as elsewhere
into the library

if I knew which volume rhythm appears in
rhythm would appear in
a square of light

COMMENTARY

On some days you can see the edges
you seem to have solved that problem with the cord
and look how the bottles fit on the shelf
even the voices calling in the street

are intended for you
and you listen for advice
because let's face it
the leaves are signs,

the lamp signifies a change
not an object in itself
although it sat for years
on the edge of the dresser

and cast a multicolored light
onto a white doily
the trees, on the other hand,
have no such permanence

they replace air every second
as they consume shape
size and quantity
to say that they "need" water

is to step out of yourself
as a man having a dream
is inclined to fly
clearly impossible

let's have the next slide
the ear actually occurred
hearing the rain on the roof
in the middle of night

he felt the room spin in circles
so that closing his eyes
saw a sea by day unstable
by night, waking

was a table of black
the way a cube
defines a jellyfish existence
this day

I learned the principle of windows
which tomorrow will seem again a wall
but between them this line
draws the arrow to N

and weights a fable

with the plumb of something seen

the yellow umbrella in the corner

is one such example

WORDS WITHOUT HISTORY

I'm on the far shore looking back
what preceded is none of my concern
what lies ahead is someone else's idea

and despite the sign
WHAT YOU CARRY CAN BE REPLACED
OTHERS HAVE DIED IN ITS CREATION

I don't mind carrying the load
the landscape is bound to be flat
never having been allowed to grow

never having wanted
not to be itself
and lacking connectives between be

and itself makes each journey shorter
than the last, no doubt to others
I appear flat as well

visible from the front
where they hang my name
but from the side

I am an "I" etched against black
almost invisible except for the quotes
that form a halo around

the place I must be, what I say
is no longer my own
but something that grew

from the voices of others
and came to resemble them
in my face

so that I carry them with me
in a flat world without smoke or cloud
or a thin rippling stream

that saying nothing
withholding nothing
goes on ahead

and I follow

TROTH

It's not much of a choice
cut off his head with a really big sword
return next year
and he cuts off yours

forests intervene
trails lead into other trails
green stands for everything
the trail isn't

home with its turrets of gold
flags bent in the wind
recedes behind a stencil of hills
why

repeat the instructions
to the letter
to the letter
is it

a. for what the old woodman wants
b. before c.
in a sequence demanding
a cup

and what's inscribed
around its rim
he's been expecting you
and you

know his bony finger
pointing toward a spire
is all there is
of this forest

but signs are intentions
and you follow
besides she's bound
to be attractive

and it's a year later
this is the test:
to be true
not to the tale

as it becomes you
but to the choice
of losing your head
for its telling, troth

takes you to Trotsky
in a book without ideas
they deal with him from a distance
so it is written

CENTURY OF HANDS

The libido portion goes haywire
I fly off in several directions
and occur to myself
at the same time

in a number of colors, alors
I am a liquid substance
and receive letters from the sun
tiens, I believe a rock

is an intelligent machine
with designs on my inside
first the spleen
like a red tongue, then the liver

known as the bad aubergine
no one must know this
I whisper in a bent-over posture
to my mirror

and when they turn off the water
and lock all the doors
it is my books they refuse me
my map my gun

who is it has made my tongue so treacherous
that the most seductive caller
is told I am an aging widower
who has moved out of town

who plants these deceptive fungi
next to the fence
that I may be tested again and again
in the crucible of taxonomies

may he be prevented from witnessing
my nova, light pouring
out of the sky, may he
become doxa, the speech

of clerks and shopkeepers
that we become the words
for lathe and forge
pounded out of capital

I exit history through the rear
the only orifice left unguarded
what was intended for me
is a bomb in a bouquet

and I am its sender, either way
I return
as the one who opens the box
and checks the numbers

abject messenger
of that effulgence destined only for me
I make the words
dance, I make the silence

THE TERROR

When we come full circle
to the rose garden in the Imaginary
will we remember the Terror

the names whose crimes are invented
in order to have something else to kill
the king's absent face at the window

across from the dock
the names of the trains
that run on time for the first time

I think of this
when I read of the stupidity of princes
with breakfast, by midday

the stock market has made one of them rich
and part of my breakfast
has bought his lunch

and paid someone to espalier
his roses across an adobe wall
they never die, the pronouns

become so malleable
they refer to anyone
but never oneself

something must be exchanged
for the privilege of joining a word
to its source, something must not fit

for its replacement to be the wrong size
then the Terror begins
in the hot weather

when they drain all the pools
and the bidding wars keep them empty
the contractor who will inherit the earth

is figuring out how to do it
even as we speak
just listen

SONG

The bowl frames the wind song
the tree branch brackets
Mt. Tam wind comes
from the west, rustles

chimes hanging
from a limb the cat climbs
as rain begins, the line
tries to gain

on sequence, fails
to frame the window, song
makes music out of wind
sing to her this motion

neither tending toward
nor caused yet love links
bowl (a gift) with wind
it stands against

HYPOTHESIS

I began
scattered
recollected in parts of the city
the parts that remain useful

rusted shed
mossy creek bottom
deserted produce district
narrative begins

in friable youth
loses itself
in uncomfortable consonants
gh and cc, water

is an ancient hypothesis
earth floats upon it
"like a piece of wood
or other flotsam"

in my second book
the censor permits us
to see everything
I refuse rehabilitation

and leave with parents
for an undisclosed location, sand
looms large in a life made
of the opinions of others

for with dispersion
we become compound
and take on the protective coloring
the desert demands

blue heron, which is gray
great egret against green pine
grebe that ducks for crustacean
in dispersion water sounds

like everything else
a crowd of mocking boys
in the balcony and the film
about an ape carrying a helpless girl

injustice begins
in the way they tell the story
of my story
I am a monkey that coincides

with a small organ, in the telling
"I" happens
discovered among cattails
forbidden words

or the olfactory richness
of basements, something indistinguishable
from something else
is handed around under the table

PROPTER HOC

The sign of the center
mandates a center
jungles fall around it
and in the last days

we arc sure to be first
I that am a center
sustain my post at the outpost
the male of the species

will act accordingly
marking its trees, an open field
beyond the smokestacks
is the sum of its perceivers

yet a man found at the site
will be assumed to have thrown a stone
and a person found in a book
will be named as the person in the book

one could not have spoken it
but could make it resound
as though a rock
were known by its circles

or an island by its print in the sand
we needed the map at first
until we memorized the lines
the last island became a peninsula

and the river gave way
to the ocean at last
then we memorized the trees, apparently
our cries could be heard from here

as birds
the We who orders these things
will never be misunderstood again
and writes it down

but a baby born in the Dragon Year
is the commune
and will misunderstand everything
surpassing legend

if she appears in flames by night
we are the fuel
if she appears all clothed in white
we are the coal

this too falls
under the sign of the center
but she makes a sound
we don't recognize

upon which nothing serving the city
can be built
and this becomes the city
after the fact

FROM

The Arcades

1998

from "Screens"

1/27/91

These are moments,
I close the door, clank
in the colander
bottle cap, beans, potato peeler,
she wears a pink turtleneck
("I'm not your little girl; I'm Sophie!")
Technicolor format of war
("Shell! Shell! Shell!")
reports of domestic violence
from the other room,
must phone P. in town a fortnight,
friend of friend
sequence of mumbled consonants,
could be report from the front
phone L. re: meet viz. Comm.
door opens, Saturday will take BART
whisk to hair, water falling in rotunda
(an illusion?) a designed rain
to soothe business
heels click in vaulted space.

1/28/91

Chords plus pauses,
air brakes in the distance
and the acacia is a little loud
a little early, bending away
from the fence, is it offended
by proximity?
one is not in the world
but in pauses (F. strikes a chord
then walks around) of the "Golf" war,
static can be sold along with the story,
correspondent lost
and pursued; you hear clashes
as volume perimeter terminus alpha
in otherwise duration,
something marks time with flames
while something is the name of the present
like a bomb owned by both sides
and broadcasting from a bunker,
the city is and is not destroyed,
unconfirmed corpses reported rotting
in the sun,
cloud cover high fifties no rain
bottlebrush stoical keeping time.

1/29/91

Blanched green washed blue
statice on the mend, earnest
purple pom-poms, air war stymied
by apparent collusion, generals stumped,
school bus turns down boulevard,
water truck air brakes alert dogs,
Mr. Noggs grumbles near the fence
(dull thunk on porch),
landform awaits its yellow flags
defines cat door or confrontation
with Norma over encroaching vines,
private colleges on endowments
defend Machiavelli
and the elder Pliny against film theory,
alert bird hops on fence, blast
of yellow almost knocks him over,
Islam is a desert with breaking news
line of soft gray scrub
declines east to supermarket
complex hidden from view.

1/30/91

Windows windows windows
school bus climbing the gradual hill
the phrase searches a phrase for what
discompletes it, start again;
incessant cough interrupts the dream,
we are having "six" in a public space
a seventh enters heaven to watch, I wake,
the suburbs wake, break the final seal,
it says
our leaders roundly applaud our leaders,
the intention to seek something large
and yellow, phrases
are given latitude, planes take off,
Sophie sees a silver wing, says
it is her father,
9:00 sun arrives at fence, acacia bows
kindly toward the east, a feather
in the form of a pen bearing the name
of Pushkin, the building called
the House of a Thousand Windows
also called Narcissus.

1/31/91

The sentence places in a rhythm of things
things that replace others,
thus are we found and yellow,
without leaves
the plum reveals the fence, the fence
birds, the birds circle up
from the junior high, the bus (yellow) leaves,
Sophie, give me some words:
"Words."
Can you give me some more words?
"More words."
Like saying the universe
is made of light, names of the intervals
names of the particles in ascending waves
(hydrogen loves oxygen)
thus was a rhythm of numbers perfected
that began as space,
the general itemizes their losses
and projects a village as ours,
the press can read the sentence
they have left room for,
necessity of weaving
if it stops the burning of voices
remains weaving
as in hair.

2/5/91

Last night I am downtown without bathroom
and people in the streets
seek shelter in laundry boxes, coffee
is getting harder to find,
the greatest danger is becoming separate
and thus equal to the buildings
in which water has been drained
leaving only sleep in a doorway,
we wake level and exhausted; in these lines
I compare my love to my car, my skis
my electrical appliance, in another
I am prone in my dorm and crave yogurt,
trees confuse February with spring
bursting in freshets of white,
we awake with a bad comparison:
the flour for cereal offering
the unleavened bread cooked in a pan
the offering mixed with oil
for which praise praise itself
has lost its voice in the desert.

Neal: "It remains a target-rich environment"
myoporum encroaches on acacia
yellow becoming dust,
gray drone parameters rotate an axis
of calibrated defense, several gain access,
others wait in sun; sandstorms, religious holidays
and transmission intersect in manor house
from ninth century bristling with antennae
Angles bearing guttural consonants
meet flagellant Saxons in documents
plant root crops thence the Venerable Bede
and ecclesiastical law,
source of income for generations,
privet hedge rises above window ledge
while Murphy scratches around dry food,
domestic landscape largely audible
largely foodstuffs: farina, dried legumes, and fruit,
an occasional sentence in early spring
takes note of its predecessors
begins to sound normal
as a tree through a window gains
leaves loses bloom.

2/12/91

Out of the bunker slash shelter target
brown lumps of hair and matted clothing
on stretchers, red brown red orange,
what distinguishes the body
without a word from other bodies
is a lolling of flesh, head hanging
over the edge
while all around, bodies tensed with purpose
lift, point, and dig; cut to Cheney
cut to Neal behind rostrum, cut to
commander in the field saying his
words; go lonely verse
to that capacious versus of thought
where blackened flesh of children hangs
like ghost laundry, surround gently what
these bytes have left behind, be balm
out of bomb, salve out of salvo,
tear out eucalyptus on the hill
that earth return
in new forms, burn
the wood later, but bodies burned in the name
of words return in forms impossible to say
and bereft of home, to these spaces
go and make miserable life listen.

2/15/91

Long night waiting at Emergency
for tiny bottle,
woke warm, cool gray
screen sky, one plane flies west
against it
George pulls up
starts Weedwacker
gulls in spiral fan out
over the Triple A, are we vast
and serene as these columns claim
or portable, a box
made of cardboard
to hold letters,
Sophie's sore spreads
across her chin
I apply salve
but walls several meters thick
contained the blast
sent bodies flying through space,
the children could not be recognized
except for their size.

2/22/91

I prefer not to say we are killing other people
I prefer to say we are servicing a target
(Bravo Battery Commander Nichols)
as in filling a tank or taking care of John
in the Men's, as in we're a service economy,
Rust Belt factories sunk in red snow
lake glittering in the distance,
librarian in Dearborn boots up Babylon
(how may I help?)
investments kept subportfolio
available upon request
polite market offers incentives
controls pollution by making it expensive
you can buy a new car with a black duck
we are a nice, disturbed culture
many centuries old, honeycombed temples
to sun, moon, and other attractions,
we are a soft target
for a male rhino urgent product straining
within central control; patience
plus language is a form of address
so small even money seems disinterested
and then we shoot.

2/25/91

Silver quilted truck serves coffee
by the almost-completed firehouse
guys in hats sit on bumpers
dusty pickups down to the corner;
you can extend this two ways: outward
from the construction site (story)
or downtown where real estate
checks the screen (system),
Boulez crash plonk, George
sights along white plastic pipe,
lays in groove, inserts drip heads,
death averted through structure
Mrs. Winchester, heiress and table rapper,
adds rooms, cool eye
attaches tube to faucet, damp patches form
by the dusty miller, line of men
hands on head
stretch to the horizon (oil fire cloud),
if there is no earth to scorch
a fire by that name burns in the head
that "hive of subtlety,"
in whose construction
the West forgets its name
turns on the water
and waits for spring.

2/28/91

The war ends and the rain begins
and begins to end,
jay's breast feathers ruffle
in a stiff wind, intermittent squalls
what's left is analysis,
troop flank deploy berm oil cost
of the small expended words, long
guns kids ride in Kuwait City
our disinterested flowing water, settling in ruts
or sheeting streets,
wet screen through which a blurred garden
seems to flow, doorbell rings, someone
wants work, something
leaves with me that is not the cat,
we are responsible for pronouns abused
in our name, that there be markets abroad
to water lawns at home, that there be others
to take my place, Sophie wakes with horses
turning on windmills, someday, she says,
we'll ride 'em.

from "The Arcades"

FORECLOSURE

An intention to whiteness
removal of the frame
removal of the sky and its border
where the flat of Kansas meets the flat
placed there, one is put
out of sight that a tilt sight
with distant silo, cloud flanked
and field
might remember position,
the placement sound,
and sense voice without angle equaling
a barn slumped into earth, hay spilled
in a blank field, the foreclosed
and tenantless grid
that an intention to whiteness
writes back, resists.

AGENCY

The eye is a product of history reproduced by education.
—PIERRE BOURDIEU

Waking in thick system
replaced with a questionnaire
or planted with readout:
apple = not salesclerk

analogy to Hyatt explains height
while product is dispensed on cards,
person is in the "up" mode
sings Gershwin unconscious toothpaste
person is colored square
heart among three pears, three *n*'s

    the NUL that was childhood
    the NUL that buys first television
    the NUL that serves breakfast
takes on the tray bearing posture of service

dream of Horowitz on tour
noodling over the Transcendentals
slice of the Berlin Wall
next to Nordstrom

I forget having come or appointment
I blank on the linkup or makeover, simply
rectify choice as representative
and send bill

     as buy
     so bought.

CORRESPONDENCE

He conceived the plan of bringing two Persians to Paris where they would conduct amazement through their letters on occasional subjects. His subject is a book seemingly empty of opinions. On this point, we have constructed a fiction based on a city the size of a city. The distinction is telling. Plot is an enticement to elaboration, governed by a square on which stands a column dedicated to those fallen in its construction. The fashionable shops on its perimeter betray an Italian locution. We exchanged letters for handbags.

I woke quirky and vague among seagulls and silvery tuna. Limp bouillion pulsates in the dining car. Had I arrested sequence in the pursuit of a stable regime or would the display of handicrafts supplement a palpable boredom? The seraglio becomes a domestic version of the despotic state, just as this fetid car describes a religious intention. I hardly know where to begin and thus conclude.

A gelatinous archaism penetrates the Hotel Chopin at the end of a corridor of glass in which I am reflected among corsets and hosiery. Perhaps we have become these reticules trimmed in ermine, but I yearn for a pictographic writing. The age demands a stereoscope with candids of temples, pyramids, and the spring beater. Implicitly our letters attack the state of frozen desserts while the cordial format invites penetration. Our empire is warmly regarded as necessary to their urban design. I await our experience with anticipation.

DISORDER

Labeling my disorder helped make it more real.
—KAREN O'CONNER

These pointed fronds wave from a glazed cachepot
amber liquid beckons to become more
than I have dressed in the audacity of,
interest mounts; they need me
mirrors need me, the new fibers
imported crushed, tensile, a person
will arrest in the act
of secreting on her person through the ruse
of a mounded issue
unnecessary objects attached to an image,
helpless before marbled and distracted planes
as "sick" becomes motto this cincture measures,
plants in the libido
until shoes address themselves
and the lapel adjusts to suit a margin,
I am as these models indicate wearable
nor has the volume
been kept low on purpose
just that in muttering a crowd will seem
to act without will and smiling.

DRAFTS

May not be letters at all
As fiery birds through a forest or indecipherable
On [upon?] the triumphant powers of Fraud
and Wrong, meanwhile I Endure
(on "tempest-scorning eagles with cedars" see . . .)

the hand tests a new quill
and at the base repeated profiles,
may be random letters or the trace
of something horizontal,
now a fire
from which sparks fleeing animals, thunderous sun
rising above freeway and the news
a businessman is stabbed in his groceries (Japan?)

erect and perfect and walking forth
but not passionless
waking and writing in the economy
while his postcard ("ordinary and / sublime relations")
returns commerce ("aureole and blue")
of a fundamental endurance

few pages reach fair copy
but remain mortal in the attempt.

EXPOSITION

The silhouette of a person who escapes us. Seen from the side she is a repetition of x's, the one to whom a letter is pointed. A classical figure facing the future as a point of defense or a port of departure, a four-gated city marked by railroads. In her hoops and bustles she is kept endlessly circulating, never sitting. Clothing becomes flowers. He intersects with metal, mobility without progress. She wears a social order, hat upon broomstick, sabots thrown into machines. Thus the union was born of a series of nouns, poorly defined positions modified by exchange. She is turned into triangles, "walking bells"; she becomes a movable type.

At a certain point they discover boredom, an index of collective sleep. Mimed by machines that seem to whirr with a divine detachment one aspires to become a balloon. One floats above fountains worked by an invisible steam engine, fountain in the shape of dolphins, shells, and aquatic plants.

We fall away from ourselves, drifting in and out of sleep, occasionally waking to wave a small flag. Upon waking we are already a moving crowd, able to be read. Observing the crowd from the standpoint of a Russian novel we gradually become a conveyance, a position, a plural. Something seen.

GENTRIFICATION

Seek remedies in the sleep margin
invisible men drinking and slouching
in transitional downtown, one
dances along a pediment on the second floor
another watches from below,
to be in their threadbare
there must be electronic gadgets
in open-air arcades, portable remedies
in the parking corridor
where the corner meets
another corner, accounts anticipate
these consumers in the big ledger
injections of an otherwise effluent
of a profitable share, the blip
is a rentable vantage from which a pitched
ball becomes a Ford
while a struck glare and bombed basement
disappear from the front page
inconsequential as a mental recently released,
read these as an imperative attachés
to luxury and intersections
will suggest themselves
much as a city creates signage
to give access to access.

INTENTION

Ruling out intention
tennis shoe options nailed in Mumbai
and sold without fanfare in Compton
it's raining lightbulbs
activewear third floor
these franchise in the salmon zones
flanking boulevards, purple medians
of agapanthus, frail and stooped.

Statistically viable on pension
negotiate walk sign by the tire store
and supplement with sheer product
pavement and turn signals blazing at noon,
transient, loose, and signless,
peering through glass at a cordless phone
cans of flat latex in pyramid
remain cool, hat reads logo.

Until an excessive intention donates a sign
Large Free Drink Fries Riot
turns off-ramp into enterprise, the Chamber
lights a smokestack and hugs table.

MAPPING

In one way all shoppers may be cruising grammarians.
—MEAGHAN MORRIS

Back of the front lay something black
peopled with familiars clothed in such
or actions stuffed with portent: point
and a person shuffles, buy
and a stranger smiles,
in this arranged and portioned glass
one finds the known, the vestige
of a lived that can be carried
in a marked sack to the next
western village with ice rink
hill town with subterranean pool
parking with vegetables; a woman
pushing a pram is snapped
from an eye in the roof, image developed
in a humming room she is not permitted
to see, but in strolling
not buying
extends, complicates these aisles
until meanders seem pointed
where upon waking for a brief
moment one is lost

save your receipt.

PAMPERS

Following the verdict
clothing seems to fall from racks
under starched neon,
a boot through a window
brings a phone to the corner
to hear glass, shouting of hightops
in a glow at the edges
that creeps closer to a toaster
or vista of infinite diapers
in Concordia near inevitable yogurt;

nothing is impervious to wear
when a collective mannequin
buys better hair,
yellows shade to browns
until we are last year's plaid,
pastels have returned
and the logo given a fresh coat,
these enterprise forget waste
when defined as product,
in the all-night sale
we can recover everything

I am lost in aisles.

PARABLE

These books are essential
on the blank of us among ads
and the effect of a novel
on white consumption,

often writing merges:
Jane and James share suds,
on a verso
is written their ardor

ego loves ego, arcadian chair
addresses gazebo
in a sequence of washed frieze,
the retreat from Pompeii

the advance on Herculaneum
as a history of ash
with excessive explosion
among emerging banks

as dunes become ribs
in a shrinking blank
lit by an installed
and foreshadowed sun,

"her people
    are patronized by ranchos
    and mañana," a metaphor
    on the recto

    describes something these books say
    is tomorrow and useful
    like the train of reason
    leaving the station of class

    from the farm of agency
    I was once the happy subject of
    and bearing sun looked up,
    couldn't read

    and wrote
    these furrows.

RECOMBINATION

I think I reticulate
among the harsh sentences,

an alphabet of subjects breeds
in a formerly white and hyperbolic,

speaking of the rubber check,
porous pocket and other political
our Chair declares null
the liberal pail, water
is 50 percent possible
in a possible chair,

we squeak following the airbrush,
Don pumps for interpretation
scattering the seemingly permanent
and stocking the mildly plural
against vestigial by noon,

turning back into cyburbia
I write Dick for an offprint
of the "Unknown Entrepreneur"
fortunes of the mildly exasperated
inspire trust
while resting in the plausible primitive,

in that form of alienation
bells announce quarters,
we wake continually in a revived
if antiseptic rural

not sleeping in the recombinant city
is like sleeping anywhere else.

RESENTMENT

First reign in Arcadia, second starched in panopticon. The gross seer packs a sack with spatulas, slotted spoons while the lesser temporizes on metropole. Requisite shepherds hard by hayrick and ruined weir, water still at the brim films over at edge, descends. Beneath pane swim glazed trout, ceramic angler casts thread in several arcs attracting flies. In this dream they are fearful of crowds prefer doorways and the love hotel, small cubicles of progress save parcels lovers covet.

Fashioned into cunning time, space seems to improve: first the swain in buskins then the agent with yellow dray, then the writer of epistles in couplet. The scheme braces for apotheosis as the streets lose their dust. Sewers improve congestion with each successive reign. Science leavens at the science fair. In the other dream he is waiting for you in a crowd, discerns a yellow dress; she smiles and the crowd parts like someone familiar. From a distance the masses resemble copper poppies waving at a priest. Disruptions of the display, purple and headless mannequins in the spring line. He stoops to peer at Spenser in the window, glass stares back from the Mutabilities in alluring nods and becks. The word's fair ornament whom this bower sells at two-pounds-eight's a shelter maze and sky.

TAPEVOICE

Here in the tentative machine first forays
into self as stretched skin
port negative seeks rudder first woman swims channel
second summer boots password I buy wherever
link terminals with alpha blunt warning
open files or die (flags wave
air bogs down in the Midwest, kisses baby)
certain commands are parallel like weep
and rain, season has a fuck option,
messages return with intention to embrace,
we are optimistic as we escape security
strategic use of humidity guns nervous
another goes unmentioned, "I" am in index
substitute imperative "purchase new files"
wait ten weeks pay supplement
achieve green life, "Bob" refers to card
which placed releases barrier, horns honk
screen darkens with impressions while truck
beeps backing this free commercial
and generous coastal scrub now grid
is subjective,
voice repeats Cheerios, oh
I pronounce these vowels as if
my own.

TRANSCRIPTION

Had been dreaming in the arcades. Attempted to dial but fingers were thumbs, eyes blunted to numbers. The odd neighbor writes again. Finds us out after twenty years with his unusual hand. Crawl spaces revisited in an epiphany of penmanship. Went down to the mall in a vestigial intention, ordered the Arlington Storage Building. Flipped through fliers for insulation and protective screen. Parent was livid. Tried to convince, but Time is a Ford.

No one prepared us for the loneliness of children. A cry in the dark, some hulking shape out of Goya. Old wedges of night: screen door banging behind restaurant, marble-top galley table, brick and board. In a page, reading and sleeping all day. Maybe catch some waves in the morning glass off. They say interesting things like actually and dinosaur.

Toxic flood plain with a smile, the old restitution of hands, work as a measure of pleasure. One wakes to hear sunset confused with rain-bow. "She" becomes "her" as the agent of possession. Her doesn't want these clothings with sleeves. These emporia represent us looking in. We learn to possess our bodies, language, the god of fire, the god of substitutions. A man gesturing in his Ford is selling a boat to no one present. Someone wakes in suburbia and needs something.

TRANSITION

The brown silence of an overstuffed apartment
slightly moist below the garden
in which we find the iris lamp
and the glass hand,

yet we love to make ourselves complex,
to twist and straighten, torment language
as though a body were a piano and the soul
a panorama of whirring wheels,

these tormented dreams of infinite city
with their conveyances forged
in a hell decorated with grapes
are erased through psychology
and a four-minute egg, toast
slightly browned,

the Gallery of Machines
flanked by plants, banks of orchids
where turbines conceive
a second Eden,

what I have lost in conversation
I send forth
in glass and steel,
fantastic lens of the present.

TRANSMISSION

for Robert Duncan

A forest or a field. Am I in the reading or is it reading me? Light through the fence, vapor lifting. Into the clearing for a better look. A lake that turned into a meadow. First field, first fealty. Then I learned how to read errancy, tracing the lips moving before the sound forms. Which eye sees me and which the wall behind, which bear is a weir bear? The unutterable cadence as a wave or train swept up in these intentions of light. A soul living through speech. Then came the age of the tape recorder. No word is crossed out; everything lives and is holy. Seeing across Lake of the Woods I was more than myself; I was called sight. Exasperation with the luggage, with the tickets in the multiple pockets, with the electrical connection and its instructions—more than himself speaking. Metal iris casts multiple yellows on a round table. In its halo an occasion for company, the cut-glass vase, the pewter creamer among the company. Present and speaking.

ZOMBIES

Moving on to policy
blue lights at the boulevard palpitate
through blank air
prodding a sleeper
into restless jeremiad,
shoppers in shirt sleeves
guys with yellow stakes
furnish civic with a warehouse
first logo then buy shares;

I was in malls
friends were buying wallets and guns
as normal music pumped
through the narcissus corridor,
teens were contagious by telephones,
what is improved is the passive
while banks make silent, soothing speech,
those had been ghosts,
now with earrings
and biceps of money become text;

waking in a jungle
the owner ponders agency
was I dream or camp stove, are these

hollows infinite with mortgage

and fifteen years, the shapes clamoring for flesh

are actually money seeking heat

they spy you emerging from accessories

like a fresh wind

and follow you to the elevator.

TRANSLATION (AFTER BAUDELAIRE)

Against the black sea of a black night
a single light
of the duty-free shop, blazing
on a broadcast horizon;
all the drowned sailors
are restored by its siren;

Desert becomes lawn, old neighborhoods
are an allegory one steps through,
the predictable and repeated windows
filled with the glass of novelty
that by wearing become new
as a pilgrim arrives refreshed in Jerusalem;

I think of you, hapless shopper
stepping through mirrors with a map of Troy
only to find yourself
frozen in representation like a swan
in Audubon, dead sweaters
roam the aisles searching for lost husbands;

Within the cloacal streets of the old city
that gather like phlegm in the throat
new boulevards form in the mind

of a white architect nearing the end
of a life spent
among the dark consonants, the mass;

We would be signs
dragging once-snowy plumage
through ravaged construction sites
that progress raise visible portions of itself
to explain the benefits of speed,
the violet frisson of acceleration;

Where was Africa,
someone in an office of tusks
on the fourteenth floor asks
and in the absence of palms and musk
a museum of masks retains these black
distances behind protective glass;

In the aisles of exile
I think of forgotten sailors
who search the horizon for a solid thing,
when wings are signs of harbor
frozen like script in azure
and bring back junk for the stalls.

from "Chronic"

YOU WERE SAYING

almost immediately
I will approach boredom
not the same
as a thinking stone

now
all of the diversions
have become
single, in the pool

falls in the ear
unlike
the phone anybody
might verify

one hears with the bones
a body dissolving
floats as if torn
by saying her name

J.
she lives by the canal
where at one
the ships glide past

or her name is broken
in boredom
the bridges raise
and the ships sail

under the word for mis-
fortune
everything is erased
or null

as the city sleeps
we begin again at five
nothing emerges from the mist
yet we see light

until what is said
is regarded as such
in the factory

to swim to convince
I feel sleepy
in the conference

in the lecture
where I am not reading
but filtering water
as an anemone is said
to breathe

an interruption
of evidence
that to recommence
hardly notices

we will meet
by the bridge
having used these words
not as a crowd

but an interested party
the phone is felt
as its words
so we say

in the reading
until glass forms
against transparency
a ringing in the ear
not an eruption

of the poem
but the sound
of water sloshing in an ear
in which a crowd

appears
at the place become familiar
and often
but several persons

in the square
a column casts its shadow
on those who died
in its honor

FOOTNOTE: ENTHYMEME

If it be great praise
to please evil men
but necessary
in which the new

to please good men
is unfortunate
given a square
of which the novel

becomes a film
of novelty
performed there
a missing term

speaks of proportion
but the action
performed there
that proves its opposite

proves we are living
a man with a home
decrees the unfortunate
leaving dung

even if homeless
we become bored
as horses
in a private yard

this is one example
a stable home
is not a premise
for one in the wide world

of which privacy is the nature
and a door
opens into squalor
alone or in numbers

something cannot be discovered
even though we had looked
every day for a week
on our way to the lake

a key in the grass
gleams
when not looking
we saw something unexpected

and picking up
opened a door
that has learned
the lake

what had been lost
familiar to a hand
expects what comes to be
parallel to the lock

a mirror in the morning
and the reflection disturbed
in our diving through
is not mine

that in itself owns nothing
agency
is not freedom
to say anything

THE AUTOBIOGRAPHY PROJECT

I is a desk
I could also be writing my life
Their Desire Is My Concession

then came the erasers
a lyric meant something
men wore hats

I couldn't write this
without a voice
I contracted into a fetus
and blew myself
back to the Neocene

there were vessels
crossing the page
the pain of the rowers
was compared
to the pain of a new nation,

the nation is a desk
with some beads and masks for support

blip germ plasma genetics perception

give this man some water
and the question of perception was
(this is the good part)
am I getting closer to you

bombs bursting, the Trilateral Commission
COINTELPRO (verdant pampa)
area studies, the invention of philology
and is "is" the subject
or an excuse to repeat functions
I secrete, I confess,

the man wearing a pumpkin
had written his memoirs,
we are were all writing ours
reading each others' for the dates

I pressed her into print
behind the Crowbar, she forced
me into a taxi in front of Plumb Bob

I keep returning to this scene
in whatsitsname
in which whatshername meets the guy
that played the lead in . . .

he had been cleared of his earlier crimes
and was warmly welcomed into Argentina

there was a colony of lepers
among whom he lived unnoticed
gradually losing his past
until all that was left . . .

I repeat am not the votary
of words as such
nor of surfaces
though others have so concluded

the public has been erased

that summer we explored the docks
in shorts, television
was on TV, he was just a placeholder
"endlessly signifying"

like as morph so glyph or look

because to look is to act
or the other way around
then came the Marshall Plan
and the walnut console

body hair and fluids
were in the distance
I was never fondled in the gym

but Indochina was
on the map, see these islands
and you think of water,
see these targets . . .

he emerged from the bunker
a quote from the Vedas already
in place, God

makes me do bad things

RULES OF CONSTRUCTION

In the present
will be understood past and future
in man
will be understood the other sex
in the third
the first turns into a stone
the second has escaped into vapor
and the sequence will include the sequence.

A camera placed at the entrance
will show that a worker
can be seen coming as going
if he enters
at the time of the explosion
his body is an exception
which you can see in exhibit E.

When the machines hum under the lagoon
the desert will seem to grow
of its own volition
the volunteers will merge with orchids
until a system under glass
will exchange carbon in a vacuum
with the other stuff
Dante proves this
with his image of . . .

POLYP

This summer they are replacing the voice
with consonants performed by lips and tongue

that penetrate your mouth when we speak
and find ourselves in what sound furthers

then the anemone opens, flutters, and folds around
the sound of water, the letter five

I can't pronounce these silences without damaging
us, the little phonemes we practice

before replacing the receiver
what else is the voice for if not the social

bodied like blips on a grid
so that if an island is invaded by sound

language is waiting to speak it into hats
and medals; I read the paper silently

not believing anything, but "we" seems to be speaking
in its vowels, the *U* into which everything pours

the *A*, foreign to myself, on a good day
I remember the infractions clearly as a ship

on a good day something has been written
and speaks back.

THE CANAL

I'd be gone with the dark sounds
gurgling in the canal,
the ones they let glide past the bridges
and the vowels that no one misses
since verging on wind, and of course
I would achieve perfect solitude,
myself and the music,
by men who have lost their hearing
in order to write the late quartets;

I am submerged, the speakers
tickling every orifice as I swim past,
rocks clicking
in an undulant billiard,
or those gray hulks
out of Shakespeare looming up
against the dock,
or could be the heart andante
in a vault of which this silent typing
is a scant record,
but one persists, turns up the volume
and thinks of the neighbors,
their eros a matter of conjecture
as I train the lens on you, auditor

auditorium, athenaeum
as I rise from the depths
for the first time, unspeakable,
and start over.

COLOPHON

Bleed Through was designed at Coffee House Press,
in the historic Grain Belt Brewery's Bottling House
near downtown Minneapolis. The text is set in Bembo.

COFFEE HOUSE PRESS

The mission of Coffee House Press is to publish exciting, vital, and enduring authors of our time; to delight and inspire readers; to contribute to the cultural life of our community; and to enrich our literary heritage. By building on the best traditions of publishing and the book arts, we produce books that celebrate imagination, innovation in the craft of writing, and the many authentic voices of the American experience.

Visit us at coffeehousepress.org.

FUNDER ACKNOWLEDGMENTS

Coffee House Press is an independent, nonprofit literary publisher. Our books are made possible through the generous support of grants and gifts from many foundations, corporate giving programs, state and federal support, and through donations from individuals who believe in the transformational power of literature. Coffee House Press receives major operating support from Amazon, the Bush Foundation, the Jerome Foundation, the McKnight Foundation, from the National Endowment for the Arts—a federal agency, from Target, and in part from a grant provided by the Minnesota State Arts Board through an appropriation by the Minnesota State Legislature from the State's general fund and its arts and cultural heritage fund with money from the vote of the people of Minnesota on November 4, 2008, and a grant from the Wells Fargo Foundation of Minnesota. Coffee House also receives support from: several anonymous donors; Suzanne Allen; Elmer L. and Eleanor J. Andersen Foundation; Around Town Agency; Patricia Beithon; Bill Berkson; the E. Thomas Binger and Rebecca Rand Fund of the Minneapolis Foundation; the Patrick and Aimee Butler Family Foundation; the Buuck Family Foundation; Claire Casey; Ruth Dayton; Dorsey & Whitney, LLP; Mary Ebert and Paul Stembler; Chris Fischbach and Katie Dublinski; Fredrikson & Byron, P.A.; Sally French; Anselm Hollo and Jane Dalrymple-Hollo; Jeffrey Hom; Carl and Heidi Horsch; Alex and Ada Katz; Stephen and Isabel Keating; Kenneth Kahn; the Kenneth Koch Literary Estate; Kathy and Dean Koutsky; the Lenfestey Family Foundation; Carol and Aaron Mack; Mary McDermid; Sjur Midness and Briar Andresen; the Nash Foundation; the Rehael Fund of the Minneapolis Foundation; Schwegman, Lundberg & Woessner, P.A.; Kiki Smith; Jeffrey Sugerman and Sarah Schultz; Patricia Tilton; the Archie D. & Bertha H. Walker Foundation; Stu Wilson and Mel Barker; the Woessner Freeman Family Foundation; Margaret and Angus Wurtele; and many other generous individual donors.

ART WORKS.
arts.gov

MINNESOTA
STATE ARTS BOARD

TARGET.

amazon.com

To you and our many readers across the country,
we send our thanks for your continuing support.

in the on the autopsy table
we kiss, mouth open,
mouths, try to evase the plural
take pleasure on the slow heat, the steady
clack of teeth
hands
magnetic pulse, two fingers on carotid artery,
something to prove they will not
identify us by
dental records, dog tags, leave
no remains
bodies flying high above cadavers

apologies in a minor key
ask the last time
i was sorry, saddened, apologies apocalyptic
no false prophets in the land
Orpheus sang his sweet song for
someone much lovelier than
Marie Antoinette paid for the privilege
of birthrights
and somehow ascension is achieved among
beer bottles and filled prescriptions
no space left on skin to be
beautiful
with a mouth dripping steel
the world will look at me and
i will look back

MICHAEL DAVIDSON is professor of literature at the University of California–San Diego. He is the author of *The San Francisco Renaissance: Poetics and Community at Mid-Century* (Cambridge University Press, 1989), *Ghostlier Demarcations: Modern Poetry and the Material Word* (University of California Press, 1997), *Guys Like Us: Citing Masculinity in Cold War Poetics* (University of Chicago Press, 2003), and *Concerto for the Left Hand: Disability and the Defamiliar Body* (University of Michigan Press, 2008). His most recent book, *Outskirts of Form: Practicing Cultural Poetics,* was published in 2011 by Wesleyan University Press. He is the editor of *The New Collected Poems of George Oppen* (New Directions, 2002). He is the author of five books of poetry, the most recent of which is *The Arcades* (O Books, 1998). He is the coauthor, with Lyn Hejinian, Barrett Watten, and Ron Silliman, of *Leningrad* (Mercury House Press, 1991).

RECENT POETRY FROM COFFEE HOUSE PRESS

The Loving Detail of the Living & the Dead
Eleni Sikelianos
978-1-56689-324-4
"Electric as a lightning storm, wild as a first-growth forest, protean as fantasy's shape-shifters—that's Sikelianos's poetry, a real pleasure to read."
—LIBRARY JOURNAL

Collected Poems
Ron Padgett
978-1-56689-342-8
Gathering the work of more than fifty years, Ron Padgett's *Collected Poems* are the record of one of the most dynamic careers in twentieth-century American poetry.

COLLECTED POEMS RON PADGETT

Sing This One Back to Me
Bob Holman
978-1-56689-325-1
From West Africa to New York City, the oral tradition comes alive through collaborative storytelling with legendary griot Papa Susso.

Dance
Lightsey Darst
978-1-56689-334-3
DANCE is poetry as performance, precarious and joyful, a three-part journey through hell, earth, and paradise.

DANCE

Lightsey Darst

The First Flag
Sarah Fox
978-1-56689-326-8
". . . utterly engaging in its seductive conversational tone." —NOR HALL

Psychedelic Norway
John Colburn
978-1-56689-335-0
Psychedelic Norway takes form as site of play and a place for the rupture of expectations.

Psychedelic Norway
JOHN COLBURN

Spiral Trace
Jack Marshall
978-1-56689-327-5
"Jack Marshall is one of our unheralded masters, which *Spiral Trace* demonstrates on almost every page." —STEPHEN DUNN

Selected Poems
Mark Ford
978-1-56689-362-6 (cloth)
978-1-56689-349-7 (paper)
978-1-56689-350-3 (e-book)
"Ford's poetry is light and agile and sometimes sweet, but it also has a disconcerting way of turning sharp and naughty and even sinister."
—JOHN ASHBERY

SELECTED POEMS MARK FORD